TEACHER'S PET PUBLICATIONS

PUZZLE PACK
for
Walk Two Moons

based on the book by
Sharon Creech

Written by
Mary B. Collins

© 2007 Teacher's Pet Publications
All Rights Reserved

The materials in this packet are copyrighted
by Teacher's Pet Publications, Inc.

These pages may be duplicated by the purchaser
for use in the purchaser's own classroom.

Copying any of these materials and distributing them
for any other purpose is a violation of the copyright laws.

© 2007 Teacher's Pet Publications, Inc.
www.tpet.com

INTRODUCTION
If you already own the LitPlan for this title, this Puzzle Pack will refresh your Unit Resource Materials and Vocabulary Resource Materials sections plus give you additional materials you can substitute into the tests. f you do not already have a complete LitPlan, these pages will give you some supplemental materials to use with your own plan. There are two main groups of materials: one set for unit words (such as characters' names, symbols, places, etc.) and one set for vocabulary words associated with the book.

WORD LIST
There is a word list for both the unit words and the vocabulary words. These lists show you which words are being used in the materials and the clues or definitions being used for those words. You may want to give students a word list with clues/definitions to help them, or you may want students to only have a word list (without clues/definitions) if you want them to work a little harder. Both are available for duplication. The word lists can also be your "calling key" for the bingo games.

FILL IN THE BLANK AND MATCHING
There are 4 each of the fill in the blank and matching worksheets for both the unit and vocabulary words. These pages can be used either as extra worksheets for students or as objective parts of a unit test. They can be done individually if students need extra help or as a whole class activity to review the material covered.

MAGIC SQUARES
The magic squares not only reinforce the material covered but also work on reasoning and math skills. Many teachers have told us that their students really enjoy doing these!

WORD SEARCH PUZZLES
The word search words go in all directions, as indicated on your answer keys. Two of the word search puzzles have the clues listed rather than the words. This makes the puzzle a little more difficult, but it reinforces the material better. Two word search puzzles have words only for students who find the clue puzzles too difficult.

CROSSWORD PUZZLES
Both unit and vocabulary word sections have 4 crossword puzzles.

BINGO CARDS
There are 32 individual bingo cards for the unit words and 32 individual bingo cards for the vocabulary words. You can use your word list as a "call list," calling the words at random and marking them off of your list as you go, or you could use the flash cards by cutting them apart and drawing the words at random from a hat (or box or whatever). To make a better review, you might ask for the definition and spelling of each word as you call it out–or you could call out the definitions and have students tell you the words they need to look for on the puzzle.

JUGGLE LETTERS
The vocabulary juggle letter game is intended to help students learn the spellings of the words. One sheet has the definitions listed on it as an extra help for students who need it or to reinforce the definitions if you choose to do so.

FLASH CARDS
We've included a set of vocabulary flash cards you can duplicate, cut, and fold for your students. Some teachers make a few sets for general use by the class; others make a set for each student. Some teachers duplicate them for each student and have the students cut & fold their own. You can cut out just the words and put them in a hat, have each student pick out one word and write the definition and a sentence for that word. Students then swap words and papers, with the next student adding a sentence of his own under the last one. You can have students swap as many times as you like. Each time the student will read the sentences written prior to his own and then add a sentence. You can cut out the words and definitions separately and play "I Have; Who Has?" Each student in the room draws a word and definition. The first student says, "I have (the name of the word). Who has the definition?" The student with the definition reads it then says, "I have (the name of the vocabulary word she has). Who has the definition?" The round continues until all words and definitions have been given.

Walk Two Moons Word List

No.	Word	Clue/Definition
1.	AGENDA	One message said that everyone has his own ___.
2.	BED	This ain't our marriage ___, but it will have to do.
3.	BEN	He drew a picture of Sal as a lizard-like creature with long, black hair.
4.	BICKLE	Police sergeant Phoebe talks to about her missing mother
5.	BIRKWAY	Mrs. Partridge's son and Mrs. Cadaver's twin brother
6.	BIRTHDAY	Sal wanted to be in Lewiston by her mother's ___.
7.	BUS	It skidded off the road, killing Sal's mother.
8.	CADAVER	Phoebe thinks she murdered her husband.
9.	CAR	Sal was locked in one with her grandparents for 6 days.
10.	CHICKEN	Ben gave one to Sal.
11.	CREECH	Author
12.	DRUNK	A ___ driver rammed into Mr. Cadaver's car.
13.	FAITHFUL	Gram always wanted to see Old ___.
14.	FINNEYS	Phoebe eats dinner at this odd family's house.
15.	FIREPLACE	Sal's father uncovered one when he learned Sal's mother wasn't coming home.
16.	GRAVE	The sheriff took Sal to her mother's.
17.	HOPE	The only good thing in Pandora's box
18.	HOSPITAL	Gram had to go there.
19.	HUZZA	Gram's saying: _____ _____ (same word twice)
20.	IDAHO	The trip destination
21.	INDIANS	Gram dances with them.
22.	JOURNALS	We had no idea all the trouble they were going to cause.
23.	JUDGE	Don't ___ a man until you've walked two moons in his moccasins.
24.	LUNATIC	Name the girls give the strange boy who came to Phoebe's house
25.	MICHIGAN	Gram put her feet into this lake
26.	MIKE	The Lunatic
27.	MOCCASIN	A water ___ bit Gram.
28.	MOONS	Walk Two ___
29.	NORMAL	Maybe dying should be ___ and terrible, according to Ben.
30.	NOTE	Mrs. Winterbottom leaves one for Mr. Winterbottom saying she had to go away.
31.	PARTRIDGE	Even though she is blind, she can see everything Phoebe is doing.
32.	PHOEBE	Sal entertained her grandparents with stories about her.
33.	PIPE	It's for remembering with: peace ___
34.	PORCH	Place where the mysterious messages were left
35.	PRUDENCE	Phoebe's sister
36.	RUSH	One of the whispering words Sal heard on her trip
37.	SACRIFICES	According to Phoebe's mother, in life you have to make some ___.
38.	SALAMANCA	Sal's whole first name
39.	SIMPLE	Word Sal used to describe her father
40.	SIOUX	The Black Hills are sacred to them.
41.	SON	Mike Bickle's relationship to Mrs. Winterbottom
42.	STILLBORN	Condition of Sal's mother's baby
43.	TIRES	Sal's grandparents got arrested for stealing these in Washington D.C.
44.	TOM	He helped save Gram's life: ___ Fleet
45.	TULIPS	Sal's mother's good-bye letter says she will return before they bloom.

Walk Two Moons Fill in the Blanks 1

_____

1. Don't ___ a man until you've walked two moons in his moccasins.
2. He helped save Gram's life: ___ Fleet
3. Phoebe's sister
4. We had no idea all the trouble they were going to cause.
5. Even though she is blind, she can see everything Phoebe is doing.
6. Police sergeant Phoebe talks to about her missing mother
7. Sal's whole first name
8. The trip destination
9. Sal was locked in one with her grandparents for 6 days.
10. Word Sal used to describe her father
11. Maybe dying should be ___ and terrible, according to Ben.
12. Author
13. The sheriff took Sal to her mother's.
14. Gram's saying: _____ _____ (same word twice)
15. Condition of Sal's mother's baby
16. The only good thing in Pandora's box
17. The Lunatic
18. Phoebe eats dinner at this odd family's house.
19. Name the girls give the strange boy who came to Phoebe's house
20. A ___ driver rammed into Mr. Cadaver's car.

Walk Two Moons Fill in the Blanks 1 Answer Key

JUDGE	1.	Don't ___ a man until you've walked two moons in his moccasins.
TOM	2.	He helped save Gram's life: ___ Fleet
PRUDENCE	3.	Phoebe's sister
JOURNALS	4.	We had no idea all the trouble they were going to cause.
PARTRIDGE	5.	Even though she is blind, she can see everything Phoebe is doing.
BICKLE	6.	Police sergeant Phoebe talks to about her missing mother
SALAMANCA	7.	Sal's whole first name
IDAHO	8.	The trip destination
CAR	9.	Sal was locked in one with her grandparents for 6 days.
SIMPLE	10.	Word Sal used to describe her father
NORMAL	11.	Maybe dying should be ___ and terrible, according to Ben.
CREECH	12.	Author
GRAVE	13.	The sheriff took Sal to her mother's.
HUZZA	14.	Gram's saying: _____ _____ (same word twice)
STILLBORN	15.	Condition of Sal's mother's baby
HOPE	16.	The only good thing in Pandora's box
MIKE	17.	The Lunatic
FINNEYS	18.	Phoebe eats dinner at this odd family's house.
LUNATIC	19.	Name the girls give the strange boy who came to Phoebe's house
DRUNK	20.	A ___ driver rammed into Mr. Cadaver's car.

Walk Two Moons Fill in the Blanks 2

1. It's for remembering with: peace ___
2. Sal was locked in one with her grandparents for 6 days.
3. It skidded off the road, killing Sal's mother.
4. Don't ___ a man until you've walked two moons in his moccasins.
5. The trip destination
6. Phoebe thinks she murdered her husband.
7. Maybe dying should be ___ and terrible, according to Ben.
8. We had no idea all the trouble they were going to cause.
9. Ben gave one to Sal.
10. The Black Hills are sacred to them.
11. Mike Bickle's relationship to Mrs. Winterbottom
12. Sal's father uncovered one when he learned Sal's mother wasn't coming home.
13. According to Phoebe's mother, in life you have to make some ___.
14. Gram's saying: _____ _____ (same word twice)
15. Phoebe eats dinner at this odd family's house.
16. Sal wanted to be in Lewiston by her mother's ___.
17. He helped save Gram's life: ___ Fleet
18. This ain't our marriage ___, but it will have to do.
19. Place where the mysterious messages were left
20. Gram put her feet into this lake

Walk Two Moons Fill in the Blanks 2 Answer Key

PIPE	1. It's for remembering with: peace ___
CAR	2. Sal was locked in one with her grandparents for 6 days.
BUS	3. It skidded off the road, killing Sal's mother.
JUDGE	4. Don't ___ a man until you've walked two moons in his moccasins.
IDAHO	5. The trip destination
CADAVER	6. Phoebe thinks she murdered her husband.
NORMAL	7. Maybe dying should be ___ and terrible, according to Ben.
JOURNALS	8. We had no idea all the trouble they were going to cause.
CHICKEN	9. Ben gave one to Sal.
SIOUX	10. The Black Hills are sacred to them.
SON	11. Mike Bickle's relationship to Mrs. Winterbottom
FIREPLACE	12. Sal's father uncovered one when he learned Sal's mother wasn't coming home.
SACRIFICES	13. According to Phoebe's mother, in life you have to make some ___.
HUZZA	14. Gram's saying: _____ _____ (same word twice)
FINNEYS	15. Phoebe eats dinner at this odd family's house.
BIRTHDAY	16. Sal wanted to be in Lewiston by her mother's ___.
TOM	17. He helped save Gram's life: ___ Fleet
BED	18. This ain't our marriage ___, but it will have to do.
PORCH	19. Place where the mysterious messages were left
MICHIGAN	20. Gram put her feet into this lake

Walk Two Moons Fill in the Blanks 3

1. The trip destination
2. Gram dances with them.
3. Sal wanted to be in Lewiston by her mother's ___.
4. The only good thing in Pandora's box
5. According to Phoebe's mother, in life you have to make some ___.
6. Mrs. Winterbottom leaves one for Mr. Winterbottom saying she had to go away.
7. Even though she is blind, she can see everything Phoebe is doing.
8. Word Sal used to describe her father
9. It's for remembering with: peace ___
10. Gram always wanted to see Old ___.
11. A water ___ bit Gram.
12. Mike Bickle's relationship to Mrs. Winterbottom
13. Condition of Sal's mother's baby
14. Ben gave one to Sal.
15. We had no idea all the trouble they were going to cause.
16. Phoebe eats dinner at this odd family's house.
17. Maybe dying should be ___ and terrible, according to Ben.
18. Gram put her feet into this lake
19. Sal's mother's good-bye letter says she will return before they bloom.
20. Place where the mysterious messages were left

Walk Two Moons Fill in the Blanks 3 Answer Key

IDAHO	1. The trip destination
INDIANS	2. Gram dances with them.
BIRTHDAY	3. Sal wanted to be in Lewiston by her mother's ___.
HOPE	4. The only good thing in Pandora's box
SACRIFICES	5. According to Phoebe's mother, in life you have to make some ___.
NOTE	6. Mrs. Winterbottom leaves one for Mr. Winterbottom saying she had to go away.
PARTRIDGE	7. Even though she is blind, she can see everything Phoebe is doing.
SIMPLE	8. Word Sal used to describe her father
PIPE	9. It's for remembering with: peace ___
FAITHFUL	10. Gram always wanted to see Old ___.
MOCCASIN	11. A water ___ bit Gram.
SON	12. Mike Bickle's relationship to Mrs. Winterbottom
STILLBORN	13. Condition of Sal's mother's baby
CHICKEN	14. Ben gave one to Sal.
JOURNALS	15. We had no idea all the trouble they were going to cause.
FINNEYS	16. Phoebe eats dinner at this odd family's house.
NORMAL	17. Maybe dying should be ___ and terrible, according to Ben.
MICHIGAN	18. Gram put her feet into this lake
TULIPS	19. Sal's mother's good-bye letter says she will return before they bloom.
PORCH	20. Place where the mysterious messages were left

Walk Two Moons Fill in the Blanks 4

1. According to Phoebe's mother, in life you have to make some ___.
2. Ben gave one to Sal.
3. He drew a picture of Sal as a lizard-like creature with long, black hair.
4. Maybe dying should be ___ and terrible, according to Ben.
5. This ain't our marriage ___, but it will have to do.
6. The only good thing in Pandora's box
7. Gram's saying: _____ _____ (same word twice)
8. A ___ driver rammed into Mr. Cadaver's car.
9. Police sergeant Phoebe talks to about her missing mother
10. Gram always wanted to see Old ___.
11. Condition of Sal's mother's baby
12. Gram dances with them.
13. Name the girls give the strange boy who came to Phoebe's house
14. The trip destination
15. Phoebe's sister
16. Even though she is blind, she can see everything Phoebe is doing.
17. The Black Hills are sacred to them.
18. Don't ___ a man until you've walked two moons in his moccasins.
19. Sal's father uncovered one when he learned Sal's mother wasn't coming home.
20. Sal's whole first name

Walk Two Moons Fill in the Blanks 4 Answer Key

SACRIFICES	1. According to Phoebe's mother, in life you have to make some ___.
CHICKEN	2. Ben gave one to Sal.
BEN	3. He drew a picture of Sal as a lizard-like creature with long, black hair.
NORMAL	4. Maybe dying should be ___ and terrible, according to Ben.
BED	5. This ain't our marriage ___, but it will have to do.
HOPE	6. The only good thing in Pandora's box
HUZZA	7. Gram's saying: _____ _____ (same word twice)
DRUNK	8. A ___ driver rammed into Mr. Cadaver's car.
BICKLE	9. Police sergeant Phoebe talks to about her missing mother
FAITHFUL	10. Gram always wanted to see Old ___.
STILLBORN	11. Condition of Sal's mother's baby
INDIANS	12. Gram dances with them.
LUNATIC	13. Name the girls give the strange boy who came to Phoebe's house
IDAHO	14. The trip destination
PRUDENCE	15. Phoebe's sister
PARTRIDGE	16. Even though she is blind, she can see everything Phoebe is doing.
SIOUX	17. The Black Hills are sacred to them.
JUDGE	18. Don't ___ a man until you've walked two moons in his moccasins.
FIREPLACE	19. Sal's father uncovered one when he learned Sal's mother wasn't coming home.
SALAMANCA	20. Sal's whole first name

Walk Two Moons Matching 1

___ 1. BIRKWAY   A. Phoebe eats dinner at this odd family's house.
___ 2. CREECH   B. Gram always wanted to see Old ___.
___ 3. MICHIGAN   C. Sal's mother's good-bye letter says she will return before they bloom.
___ 4. BICKLE   D. Police sergeant Phoebe talks to about her missing mother
___ 5. AGENDA   E. Mrs. Partridge's son and Mrs. Cadaver's twin brother
___ 6. BEN   F. Gram's saying: _____ _____ (same word twice)
___ 7. STILLBORN   G. Don't ___ a man until you've walked two moons in his moccasins.
___ 8. FINNEYS   H. Author
___ 9. TULIPS   I. This ain't our marriage ___, but it will have to do.
___ 10. HOPE   J. Sal wanted to be in Lewiston by her mother's ___.
___ 11. DRUNK   K. Mrs. Winterbottom leaves one for Mr. Winterbottom saying she had to go away.
___ 12. HOSPITAL   L. The only good thing in Pandora's box
___ 13. MOONS   M. A ___ driver rammed into Mr. Cadaver's car.
___ 14. BED   N. Gram dances with them.
___ 15. HUZZA   O. One message said that everyone has his own ___.
___ 16. PARTRIDGE   P. Gram put her feet into this lake
___ 17. SIMPLE   Q. One of the whispering words Sal heard on her trip
___ 18. RUSH   R. Gram had to go there.
___ 19. JUDGE   S. Sal was locked in one with her grandparents for 6 days.
___ 20. NOTE   T. Walk Two ___
___ 21. FAITHFUL   U. Even though she is blind, she can see everything Phoebe is doing.
___ 22. INDIANS   V. Condition of Sal's mother's baby
___ 23. BIRTHDAY   W. Word Sal used to describe her father
___ 24. PORCH   X. He drew a picture of Sal as a lizard-like creature with long, black hair.
___ 25. CAR   Y. Place where the mysterious messages were left

Walk Two Moons Matching 1 Answer Key

E - 1. BIRKWAY	A.	Phoebe eats dinner at this odd family's house.
H - 2. CREECH	B.	Gram always wanted to see Old ___.
P - 3. MICHIGAN	C.	Sal's mother's good-bye letter says she will return before they bloom.
D - 4. BICKLE	D.	Police sergeant Phoebe talks to about her missing mother
O - 5. AGENDA	E.	Mrs. Partridge's son and Mrs. Cadaver's twin brother
X - 6. BEN	F.	Gram's saying: _____ _____ (same word twice)
V - 7. STILLBORN	G.	Don't ___ a man until you've walked two moons in his moccasins.
A - 8. FINNEYS	H.	Author
C - 9. TULIPS	I.	This ain't our marriage ___, but it will have to do.
L - 10. HOPE	J.	Sal wanted to be in Lewiston by her mother's ___.
M - 11. DRUNK	K.	Mrs. Winterbottom leaves one for Mr. Winterbottom saying she had to go away.
R - 12. HOSPITAL	L.	The only good thing in Pandora's box
T - 13. MOONS	M.	A ___ driver rammed into Mr. Cadaver's car.
I - 14. BED	N.	Gram dances with them.
F - 15. HUZZA	O.	One message said that everyone has his own ___.
U - 16. PARTRIDGE	P.	Gram put her feet into this lake
W - 17. SIMPLE	Q.	One of the whispering words Sal heard on her trip
Q - 18. RUSH	R.	Gram had to go there.
G - 19. JUDGE	S.	Sal was locked in one with her grandparents for 6 days.
K - 20. NOTE	T.	Walk Two ___
B - 21. FAITHFUL	U.	Even though she is blind, she can see everything Phoebe is doing.
N - 22. INDIANS	V.	Condition of Sal's mother's baby
J - 23. BIRTHDAY	W.	Word Sal used to describe her father
Y - 24. PORCH	X.	He drew a picture of Sal as a lizard-like creature with long, black hair.
S - 25. CAR	Y.	Place where the mysterious messages were left

Walk Two Moons Matching 2

___ 1.	INDIANS	A.	Name the girls give the strange boy who came to Phoebe's house
___ 2.	FINNEYS	B.	It's for remembering with: peace ___
___ 3.	BEN	C.	Gram always wanted to see Old ___.
___ 4.	LUNATIC	D.	Gram had to go there.
___ 5.	PORCH	E.	Mike Bickle's relationship to Mrs. Winterbottom
___ 6.	BIRTHDAY	F.	Mrs. Partridge's son and Mrs. Cadaver's twin brother
___ 7.	FAITHFUL	G.	One message said that everyone has his own ___.
___ 8.	PHOEBE	H.	Condition of Sal's mother's baby
___ 9.	BIRKWAY	I.	Sal entertained her grandparents with stories about her.
___10.	TULIPS	J.	Walk Two ___
___11.	NORMAL	K.	A ___ driver rammed into Mr. Cadaver's car.
___12.	SACRIFICES	L.	Phoebe eats dinner at this odd family's house.
___13.	TIRES	M.	Gram dances with them.
___14.	HUZZA	N.	According to Phoebe's mother, in life you have to make some ___.
___15.	SIOUX	O.	Sal's grandparents got arrested for stealing these in Washington D.C.
___16.	HOPE	P.	Gram's saying: _____ _____ (same word twice)
___17.	PIPE	Q.	The only good thing in Pandora's box
___18.	AGENDA	R.	The Black Hills are sacred to them.
___19.	DRUNK	S.	The trip destination
___20.	IDAHO	T.	He drew a picture of Sal as a lizard-like creature with long, black hair.
___21.	STILLBORN	U.	Maybe dying should be ___ and terrible, according to Ben.
___22.	HOSPITAL	V.	Place where the mysterious messages were left
___23.	FIREPLACE	W.	Sal wanted to be in Lewiston by her mother's ___.
___24.	MOONS	X.	Sal's mother's good-bye letter says she will return before they bloom.
___25.	SON	Y.	Sal's father uncovered one when he learned Sal's mother wasn't coming home.

Walk Two Moons Matching 2 Answer Key

M - 1. INDIANS	A.	Name the girls give the strange boy who came to Phoebe's house
L - 2. FINNEYS	B.	It's for remembering with: peace ___
T - 3. BEN	C.	Gram always wanted to see Old ___.
A - 4. LUNATIC	D.	Gram had to go there.
V - 5. PORCH	E.	Mike Bickle's relationship to Mrs. Winterbottom
W - 6. BIRTHDAY	F.	Mrs. Partridge's son and Mrs. Cadaver's twin brother
C - 7. FAITHFUL	G.	One message said that everyone has his own ___.
I - 8. PHOEBE	H.	Condition of Sal's mother's baby
F - 9. BIRKWAY	I.	Sal entertained her grandparents with stories about her.
X - 10. TULIPS	J.	Walk Two ___
U - 11. NORMAL	K.	A ___ driver rammed into Mr. Cadaver's car.
N - 12. SACRIFICES	L.	Phoebe eats dinner at this odd family's house.
O - 13. TIRES	M.	Gram dances with them.
P - 14. HUZZA	N.	According to Phoebe's mother, in life you have to make some ___.
R - 15. SIOUX	O.	Sal's grandparents got arrested for stealing these in Washington D.C.
Q - 16. HOPE	P.	Gram's saying: _____ _____ (same word twice)
B - 17. PIPE	Q.	The only good thing in Pandora's box
G - 18. AGENDA	R.	The Black Hills are sacred to them.
K - 19. DRUNK	S.	The trip destination
S - 20. IDAHO	T.	He drew a picture of Sal as a lizard-like creature with long, black hair.
H - 21. STILLBORN	U.	Maybe dying should be ___ and terrible, according to Ben.
D - 22. HOSPITAL	V.	Place where the mysterious messages were left
Y - 23. FIREPLACE	W.	Sal wanted to be in Lewiston by her mother's ___.
J - 24. MOONS	X.	Sal's mother's good-bye letter says she will return before they bloom.
E - 25. SON	Y.	Sal's father uncovered one when he learned Sal's mother wasn't coming home.

Walk Two Moons Matching 3

___ 1. MOONS A. Ben gave one to Sal.
___ 2. CADAVER B. He helped save Gram's life: ___ Fleet
___ 3. JUDGE C. The trip destination
___ 4. PRUDENCE D. Name the girls give the strange boy who came to Phoebe's house
___ 5. NOTE E. Sal's mother's good-bye letter says she will return before they bloom.
___ 6. FIREPLACE F. Phoebe thinks she murdered her husband.
___ 7. PIPE G. This ain't our marriage ___, but it will have to do.
___ 8. HUZZA H. We had no idea all the trouble they were going to cause.
___ 9. JOURNALS I. The Black Hills are sacred to them.
___ 10. RUSH J. Phoebe's sister
___ 11. LUNATIC K. Sal wanted to be in Lewiston by her mother's ___.
___ 12. STILLBORN L. Sal's father uncovered one when he learned Sal's mother wasn't coming home.
___ 13. PHOEBE M. Condition of Sal's mother's baby
___ 14. CHICKEN N. Gram always wanted to see Old ___.
___ 15. FAITHFUL O. It's for remembering with: peace ___
___ 16. MICHIGAN P. Sal was locked in one with her grandparents for 6 days.
___ 17. PARTRIDGE Q. Don't ___ a man until you've walked two moons in his moccasins.
___ 18. CAR R. Sal entertained her grandparents with stories about her.
___ 19. TULIPS S. Gram put her feet into this lake
___ 20. TOM T. Even though she is blind, she can see everything Phoebe is doing.
___ 21. BIRTHDAY U. Mrs. Partridge's son and Mrs. Cadaver's twin brother
___ 22. SIOUX V. Walk Two ___
___ 23. BIRKWAY W. Mrs. Winterbottom leaves one for Mr. Winterbottom saying she had to go away.
___ 24. IDAHO X. One of the whispering words Sal heard on her trip
___ 25. BED Y. Gram's saying: _____ _____ (same word twice)

Walk Two Moons Matching 3 Answer Key

V - 1. MOONS	A.	Ben gave one to Sal.
F - 2. CADAVER	B.	He helped save Gram's life: ___ Fleet
Q - 3. JUDGE	C.	The trip destination
J - 4. PRUDENCE	D.	Name the girls give the strange boy who came to Phoebe's house
W - 5. NOTE	E.	Sal's mother's good-bye letter says she will return before they bloom.
L - 6. FIREPLACE	F.	Phoebe thinks she murdered her husband.
O - 7. PIPE	G.	This ain't our marriage ___, but it will have to do.
Y - 8. HUZZA	H.	We had no idea all the trouble they were going to cause.
H - 9. JOURNALS	I.	The Black Hills are sacred to them.
X - 10. RUSH	J.	Phoebe's sister
D - 11. LUNATIC	K.	Sal wanted to be in Lewiston by her mother's ___.
M - 12. STILLBORN	L.	Sal's father uncovered one when he learned Sal's mother wasn't coming home.
R - 13. PHOEBE	M.	Condition of Sal's mother's baby
A - 14. CHICKEN	N.	Gram always wanted to see Old ___.
N - 15. FAITHFUL	O.	It's for remembering with: peace ___
S - 16. MICHIGAN	P.	Sal was locked in one with her grandparents for 6 days.
T - 17. PARTRIDGE	Q.	Don't ___ a man until you've walked two moons in his moccasins.
P - 18. CAR	R.	Sal entertained her grandparents with stories about her.
E - 19. TULIPS	S.	Gram put her feet into this lake
B - 20. TOM	T.	Even though she is blind, she can see everything Phoebe is doing.
K - 21. BIRTHDAY	U.	Mrs. Partridge's son and Mrs. Cadaver's twin brother
I - 22. SIOUX	V.	Walk Two ___
U - 23. BIRKWAY	W.	Mrs. Winterbottom leaves one for Mr. Winterbottom saying she had to go away.
C - 24. IDAHO	X.	One of the whispering words Sal heard on her trip
G - 25. BED	Y.	Gram's saying: _____ _____ (same word twice)

Walk Two Moons Matching 4

___ 1. JOURNALS   A. He helped save Gram's life: ___ Fleet
___ 2. BICKLE   B. Gram put her feet into this lake
___ 3. SON   C. Place where the mysterious messages were left
___ 4. SIOUX   D. Sal entertained her grandparents with stories about her.
___ 5. TOM   E. The sheriff took Sal to her mother's.
___ 6. FIREPLACE   F. Even though she is blind, she can see everything Phoebe is doing.
___ 7. CADAVER   G. The only good thing in Pandora's box
___ 8. PARTRIDGE   H. Sal's father uncovered one when he learned Sal's mother wasn't coming home.
___ 9. TIRES   I. Name the girls give the strange boy who came to Phoebe's house
___10. BEN   J. The trip destination
___11. BIRTHDAY   K. Maybe dying should be ___ and terrible, according to Ben.
___12. HOPE   L. We had no idea all the trouble they were going to cause.
___13. PORCH   M. Sal's grandparents got arrested for stealing these in Washington D.C.
___14. LUNATIC   N. Sal was locked in one with her grandparents for 6 days.
___15. BUS   O. The Black Hills are sacred to them.
___16. NORMAL   P. Sal wanted to be in Lewiston by her mother's ___.
___17. NOTE   Q. One of the whispering words Sal heard on her trip
___18. GRAVE   R. He drew a picture of Sal as a lizard-like creature with long, black hair.
___19. RUSH   S. Phoebe thinks she murdered her husband.
___20. MICHIGAN   T. Phoebe's sister
___21. SACRIFICES   U. It skidded off the road, killing Sal's mother.
___22. IDAHO   V. Police sergeant Phoebe talks to about her missing mother
___23. PRUDENCE   W. According to Phoebe's mother, in life you have to make some ___.
___24. CAR   X. Mrs. Winterbottom leaves one for Mr. Winterbottom saying she had to go away.
___25. PHOEBE   Y. Mike Bickle's relationship to Mrs. Winterbottom

Walk Two Moons Matching 4 Answer Key

L - 1.	JOURNALS	A.	He helped save Gram's life: ___ Fleet
V - 2.	BICKLE	B.	Gram put her feet into this lake
Y - 3.	SON	C.	Place where the mysterious messages were left
O - 4.	SIOUX	D.	Sal entertained her grandparents with stories about her.
A - 5.	TOM	E.	The sheriff took Sal to her mother's.
H - 6.	FIREPLACE	F.	Even though she is blind, she can see everything Phoebe is doing.
S - 7.	CADAVER	G.	The only good thing in Pandora's box
F - 8.	PARTRIDGE	H.	Sal's father uncovered one when he learned Sal's mother wasn't coming home.
M - 9.	TIRES	I.	Name the girls give the strange boy who came to Phoebe's house
R -10.	BEN	J.	The trip destination
P -11.	BIRTHDAY	K.	Maybe dying should be ___ and terrible, according to Ben.
G -12.	HOPE	L.	We had no idea all the trouble they were going to cause.
C -13.	PORCH	M.	Sal's grandparents got arrested for stealing these in Washington D.C.
I - 14.	LUNATIC	N.	Sal was locked in one with her grandparents for 6 days.
U -15.	BUS	O.	The Black Hills are sacred to them.
K -16.	NORMAL	P.	Sal wanted to be in Lewiston by her mother's ___.
X -17.	NOTE	Q.	One of the whispering words Sal heard on her trip
E -18.	GRAVE	R.	He drew a picture of Sal as a lizard-like creature with long, black hair.
Q -19.	RUSH	S.	Phoebe thinks she murdered her husband.
B -20.	MICHIGAN	T.	Phoebe's sister
W -21.	SACRIFICES	U.	It skidded off the road, killing Sal's mother.
J -22.	IDAHO	V.	Police sergeant Phoebe talks to about her missing mother
T -23.	PRUDENCE	W.	According to Phoebe's mother, in life you have to make some ___.
N -24.	CAR	X.	Mrs. Winterbottom leaves one for Mr. Winterbottom saying she had to go away.
D -25.	PHOEBE	Y.	Mike Bickle's relationship to Mrs. Winterbottom

Walk Two Moons Magic Squares 1

Match the definition with the vocabulary word. Put your answers in the magic squares below. When your answers are correct, all columns and rows will add to the same number.

A. TIRES   E. STILLBORN   I. PRUDENCE   M. MIKE
B. MICHIGAN   F. LUNATIC   J. CHICKEN   N. GRAVE
C. IDAHO   G. SACRIFICES   K. AGENDA   O. HOSPITAL
D. CREECH   H. PIPE   L. BED   P. CADAVER

1. The trip destination
2. Ben gave one to Sal.
3. Name the girls give the strange boy who came to Phoebe's house
4. Gram had to go there.
5. Phoebe thinks she murdered her husband.
6. Condition of Sal's mother's baby
7. Phoebe's sister
8. Author
9. The Lunatic
10. It's for remembering with: peace ___
11. This ain't our marriage ___, but it will have to do.
12. Sal's grandparents got arrested for stealing these in Washington D.C.
13. Gram put her feet into this lake
14. One message said that everyone has his own ___.
15. According to Phoebe's mother, in life you have to make some ___.
16. The sheriff took Sal to her mother's.

A=	B=	C=	D=
E=	F=	G=	H=
I=	J=	K=	L=
M=	N=	O=	P=

Walk Two Moons Magic Squares 1 Answer Key

Match the definition with the vocabulary word. Put your answers in the magic squares below. When your answers are correct, all columns and rows will add to the same number.

A. TIRES
B. MICHIGAN
C. IDAHO
D. CREECH
E. STILLBORN
F. LUNATIC
G. SACRIFICES
H. PIPE
I. PRUDENCE
J. CHICKEN
K. AGENDA
L. BED
M. MIKE
N. GRAVE
O. HOSPITAL
P. CADAVER

1. The trip destination
2. Ben gave one to Sal.
3. Name the girls give the strange boy who came to Phoebe's house
4. Gram had to go there.
5. Phoebe thinks she murdered her husband.
6. Condition of Sal's mother's baby
7. Phoebe's sister
8. Author
9. The Lunatic
10. It's for remembering with: peace ___
11. This ain't our marriage ___, but it will have to do.
12. Sal's grandparents got arrested for stealing these in Washington D.C.
13. Gram put her feet into this lake
14. One message said that everyone has his own ___.
15. According to Phoebe's mother, in life you have to make some ___.
16. The sheriff took Sal to her mother's.

A=12	B=13	C=1	D=8
E=6	F=3	G=15	H=10
I=7	J=2	K=14	L=11
M=9	N=16	O=4	P=5

Walk Two Moons Magic Squares 2

Match the definition with the vocabulary word. Put your answers in the magic squares below. When your answers are correct, all columns and rows will add to the same number.

A. JUDGE
B. FIREPLACE
C. PHOEBE
D. TIRES
E. CREECH
F. STILLBORN
G. TULIPS
H. PORCH
I. MICHIGAN
J. INDIANS
K. FINNEYS
L. CAR
M. PARTRIDGE
N. BIRTHDAY
O. HUZZA
P. IDAHO

1. Place where the mysterious messages were left
2. Even though she is blind, she can see everything Phoebe is doing.
3. Sal's father uncovered one when he learned Sal's mother wasn't coming home.
4. Phoebe eats dinner at this odd family's house.
5. Gram dances with them.
6. Sal entertained her grandparents with stories about her.
7. The trip destination
8. Author
9. Gram's saying: _____ _____ (same word twice)
10. Condition of Sal's mother's baby
11. Gram put her feet into this lake
12. Sal's grandparents got arrested for stealing these in Washington D.C.
13. Don't ___ a man until you've walked two moons in his moccasins.
14. Sal was locked in one with her grandparents for 6 days.
15. Sal's mother's good-bye letter says she will return before they bloom.
16. Sal wanted to be in Lewiston by her mother's ___.

A=	B=	C=	D=
E=	F=	G=	H=
I=	J=	K=	L=
M=	N=	O=	P=

Walk Two Moons Magic Squares 2 Answer Key

Match the definition with the vocabulary word. Put your answers in the magic squares below. When your answers are correct, all columns and rows will add to the same number.

A. JUDGE   E. CREECH   I. MICHIGAN   M. PARTRIDGE
B. FIREPLACE   F. STILLBORN   J. INDIANS   N. BIRTHDAY
C. PHOEBE   G. TULIPS   K. FINNEYS   O. HUZZA
D. TIRES   H. PORCH   L. CAR   P. IDAHO

1. Place where the mysterious messages were left
2. Even though she is blind, she can see everything Phoebe is doing.
3. Sal's father uncovered one when he learned Sal's mother wasn't coming home.
4. Phoebe eats dinner at this odd family's house.
5. Gram dances with them.
6. Sal entertained her grandparents with stories about her.
7. The trip destination
8. Author
9. Gram's saying: _____ _____ (same word twice)
10. Condition of Sal's mother's baby
11. Gram put her feet into this lake
12. Sal's grandparents got arrested for stealing these in Washington D.C.
13. Don't ___ a man until you've walked two moons in his moccasins.
14. Sal was locked in one with her grandparents for 6 days.
15. Sal's mother's good-bye letter says she will return before they bloom.
16. Sal wanted to be in Lewiston by her mother's ___.

A=13	B=3	C=6	D=12
E=8	F=10	G=15	H=1
I=11	J=5	K=4	L=14
M=2	N=16	O=9	P=7

Walk Two Moons Magic Squares 3

Match the definition with the vocabulary word. Put your answers in the magic squares below. When your answers are correct, all columns and rows will add to the same number.

A. BIRTHDAY E. PORCH   I. SIMPLE   M. BIRKWAY
B. HUZZA   F. IDAHO   J. MOCCASIN N. FIREPLACE
C. CHICKEN   G. INDIANS K. NORMAL   O. JOURNALS
D. HOPE   H. TULIPS   L. PIPE   P. PHOEBE

1. Sal's mother's good-bye letter says she will return before they bloom.
2. Sal wanted to be in Lewiston by her mother's ___.
3. Gram's saying: _____ _____ (same word twice)
4. Gram dances with them.
5. A water ___ bit Gram.
6. We had no idea all the trouble they were going to cause.
7. Sal entertained her grandparents with stories about her.
8. Word Sal used to describe her father
9. Maybe dying should be ___ and terrible, according to Ben.
10. Sal's father uncovered one when he learned Sal's mother wasn't coming home.
11. Mrs. Partridge's son and Mrs. Cadaver's twin brother
12. It's for remembering with: peace ___
13. Place where the mysterious messages were left
14. The only good thing in Pandora's box
15. Ben gave one to Sal.
16. The trip destination

A=	B=	C=	D=
E=	F=	G=	H=
I=	J=	K=	L=
M=	N=	O=	P=

Walk Two Moons Magic Squares 3 Answer Key

Match the definition with the vocabulary word. Put your answers in the magic squares below. When your answers are correct, all columns and rows will add to the same number.

A. BIRTHDAY   E. PORCH   I. SIMPLE   M. BIRKWAY
B. HUZZA   F. IDAHO   J. MOCCASIN   N. FIREPLACE
C. CHICKEN   G. INDIANS   K. NORMAL   O. JOURNALS
D. HOPE   H. TULIPS   L. PIPE   P. PHOEBE

1. Sal's mother's good-bye letter says she will return before they bloom.
2. Sal wanted to be in Lewiston by her mother's ___.
3. Gram's saying: _____ _____ (same word twice)
4. Gram dances with them.
5. A water ___ bit Gram.
6. We had no idea all the trouble they were going to cause.
7. Sal entertained her grandparents with stories about her.
8. Word Sal used to describe her father
9. Maybe dying should be ___ and terrible, according to Ben.
10. Sal's father uncovered one when he learned Sal's mother wasn't coming home.
11. Mrs. Partridge's son and Mrs. Cadaver's twin brother
12. It's for remembering with: peace ___
13. Place where the mysterious messages were left
14. The only good thing in Pandora's box
15. Ben gave one to Sal.
16. The trip destination

A=2	B=3	C=15	D=14
E=13	F=16	G=4	H=1
I=8	J=5	K=9	L=12
M=11	N=10	O=6	P=7

Walk Two Moons Magic Squares 4

Match the definition with the vocabulary word. Put your answers in the magic squares below. When your answers are correct, all columns and rows will add to the same number.

A. CREECH   E. MOCCASIN   I. BIRTHDAY   M. HOPE
B. CADAVER   F. GRAVE   J. MICHIGAN   N. TOM
C. SACRIFICES G. DRUNK   K. FIREPLACE   O. SICUX
D. FAITHFUL   H. BIRKWAY   L. PHOEBE   P. BUS

1. The only good thing in Pandora's box
2. The sheriff took Sal to her mother's.
3. Mrs. Partridge's son and Mrs. Cadaver's twin brother
4. The Black Hills are sacred to them.
5. Sal entertained her grandparents with stories about her.
6. According to Phoebe's mother, in life you have to make some ___.
7. Author
8. Gram put her feet into this lake
9. Sal's father uncovered one when he learned Sal's mother wasn't coming home.
10. Gram always wanted to see Old ___.
11. Phoebe thinks she murdered her husband.
12. Sal wanted to be in Lewiston by her mother's ___.
13. He helped save Gram's life: ___ Fleet
14. A water ___ bit Gram.
15. A ___ driver rammed into Mr. Cadaver's car.
16. It skidded off the road, killing Sal's mother.

A=	B=	C=	D=
E=	F=	G=	H=
I=	J=	K=	L=
M=	N=	O=	P=

Walk Two Moons Magic Squares 4 Answer Key

Match the definition with the vocabulary word. Put your answers in the magic squares below. When your answers are correct, all columns and rows will add to the same number.

A. CREECH   E. MOCCASIN   I. BIRTHDAY   M. HOPE
B. CADAVER   F. GRAVE   J. MICHIGAN   N. TOM
C. SACRIFICES G. DRUNK   K. FIREPLACE   O. SIOUX
D. FAITHFUL H. BIRKWAY   L. PHOEBE   P. BUS

1. The only good thing in Pandora's box
2. The sheriff took Sal to her mother's.
3. Mrs. Partridge's son and Mrs. Cadaver's twin brother
4. The Black Hills are sacred to them.
5. Sal entertained her grandparents with stories about her.
6. According to Phoebe's mother, in life you have to make some ___.
7. Author
8. Gram put her feet into this lake
9. Sal's father uncovered one when he learned Sal's mother wasn't coming home.
10. Gram always wanted to see Old ___.
11. Phoebe thinks she murdered her husband.
12. Sal wanted to be in Lewiston by her mother's ___.
13. He helped save Gram's life: ___ Fleet
14. A water ___ bit Gram.
15. A ___ driver rammed into Mr. Cadaver's car.
16. It skidded off the road, killing Sal's mother.

A=7	B=11	C=6	D=10
E=14	F=2	G=15	H=3
I=12	J=8	K=9	L=5
M=1	N=13	O=4	P=16

Walk Two Moons Word Search 1

```
B U S C A D A V E R F A I T H F U L
M W L F N G P H Y C M B N H V J J R
G I L I T O E J O Y H O I O L M K H
R T K R Q O T N O S T I C R R W Q L
P H O E B E M E D U P F C C K M K P
S B B P M C K S R A R I Z K A W A Z
B I I L B P T I U S U N T Z E S A L
Q C R A H O V M N L D N A A W N I Y
P K T C I R G P K U E E V L L R X N
A L H E N C P L J N N Y N H S G W Q
R E D S D H R E V A C S G S T Q T T
T T A D I H D E D T E M R M D C U W
R Y Y M A O U K E I I N A O H T L D
I Q W V N F U Z P C C R V O L O I N
D J R U S H X X Z L H B E N P I P E
G W Q B O V S W T A N Z P S N Q S E
E B E D N C A R I D A H O J U D G E
```

A ___ driver rammed into Mr. Cadaver's car. (5)
A water ___ bit Gram. (8)
Author (6)
Ben gave one to Sal. (7)
Don't ___ a man until you've walked two moons in his moccasins. (5)
Even though she is blind, she can see everything Phoebe is doing. (9)
Gram always wanted to see Old ___. (8)
Gram dances with them. (7)
Gram had to go there. (8)
Gram's saying: _____ _____ (same word twice) (5)
He drew a picture of Sal as a lizard-like creature with long, black hair. (3)
He helped save Gram's life: ___ Fleet (3)
It skidded off the road, killing Sal's mother. (3)
It's for remembering with: peace ___ (4)
Maybe dying should be ___ and terrible, according to Ben. (6)
Mike Bickle's relationship to Mrs. Winterbottom (3)
Mrs. Partridge's son and Mrs. Cadaver's twin brother (7)
Mrs. Winterbottom leaves one for Mr. Winterbottom saying she had to go away. (4)
Name the girls give the strange boy who came to Phoebe's house (7)
One message said that everyone has his own ___. (6)
One of the whispering words Sal heard on her trip (4)
Phoebe eats dinner at this odd family's house. (7)
Phoebe thinks she murdered her husband. (7)
Phoebe's sister (8)
Place where the mysterious messages were left (5)
Police sergeant Phoebe talks to about her missing mother (6)
Sal entertained her grandparents with stories about her. (6)
Sal wanted to be in Lewiston by her mother's ___. (8)
Sal was locked in one with her grandparents for 6 days. (3)
Sal's father uncovered one when he learned Sal's mother wasn't coming home. (9)
Sal's grandparents got arrested for stealing these in Washington D.C. (5)
Sal's mother's good-bye letter says she will return before they bloom. (6)
The Black Hills are sacred to them. (5)
The Lunatic (4)
The only good thing in Pandora's box (4)
The sheriff took Sal to her mother's. (5)
The trip destination (5)
This ain't our marriage ___, but it will have to do. (3)
Walk Two ___ (5)
We had no idea all the trouble they were going to cause. (8)
Word Sal used to describe her father (6)

Walk Two Moons Word Search 1 Answer Key

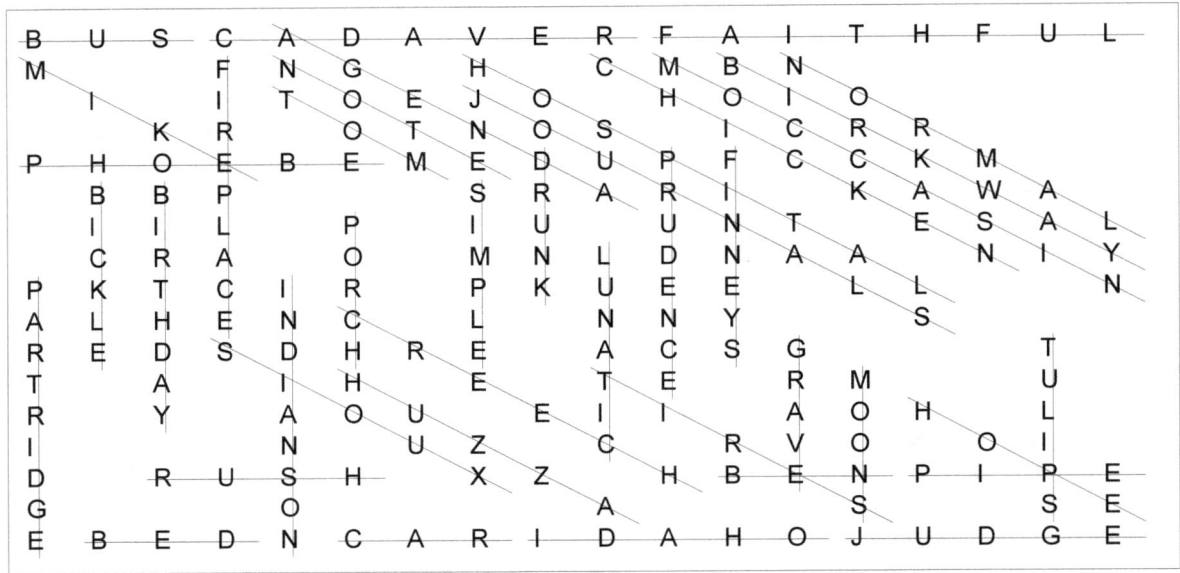

A ___ driver rammed into Mr. Cadaver's car. (5)
A water ___ bit Gram. (8)
Author (6)
Ben gave one to Sal. (7)
Don't ___ a man until you've walked two moons in his moccasins. (5)
Even though she is blind, she can see everything Phoebe is doing. (9)
Gram always wanted to see Old ___. (8)
Gram dances with them. (7)
Gram had to go there. (8)
Gram's saying: _____ _____ (same word twice) (5)
He drew a picture of Sal as a lizard-like creature with long, black hair. (3)
He helped save Gram's life: ___ Fleet (3)
It skidded off the road, killing Sal's mother. (3)
It's for remembering with: peace ___ (4)
Maybe dying should be ___ and terrible, according to Ben. (6)
Mike Bickle's relationship to Mrs. Winterbottom (3)
Mrs. Partridge's son and Mrs. Cadaver's twin brother (7)
Mrs. Winterbottom leaves one for Mr. Winterbottom saying she had to go away. (4)
Name the girls give the strange boy who came to Phoebe's house (7)
One message said that everyone has his own ___. (6)
One of the whispering words Sal heard on her trip (4)

Phoebe eats dinner at this odd family's house. (7)
Phoebe thinks she murdered her husband. (7)
Phoebe's sister (8)
Place where the mysterious messages were left (5)
Police sergeant Phoebe talks to about her missing mother (6)
Sal entertained her grandparents with stories about her. (6)
Sal wanted to be in Lewiston by her mother's ___. (8)
Sal was locked in one with her grandparents for 6 days. (3)
Sal's father uncovered one when he learned Sal's mother wasn't coming home. (9)
Sal's grandparents got arrested for stealing these in Washington D.C. (5)
Sal's mother's good-bye letter says she will return before they bloom. (6)
The Black Hills are sacred to them. (5)
The Lunatic (4)
The only good thing in Pandora's box (4)
The sheriff took Sal to her mother's. (5)
The trip destination (5)
This ain't our marriage ___, but it will have to do. (3)
Walk Two ___ (5)
We had no idea all the trouble they were going to cause. (8)
Word Sal used to describe her father (6)

Walk Two Moons Word Search 2

```
C L P B S T I R E S B M R M T W J M
H F R I I I N W K G P I O L O H U V
I M U R M K O V N R I K C O M M D P
C M D T P K R U P A P E R K N L G Z
K M E H L D M P X V E H P U L S E Y
E O N D E Q A I O E N T M H S E P S
N C C A C F L G D R B O R M O H F N
S C E Y W A I H E A C V T Z L E K R
T A A K N J D N U N H H F E U P B D
I S H R F O B A N Z D O I Y N A H E
L I M M A U I N V E Z A R C A R O D
L N V N I R R C B E Y A E R T T S X
B R X Z T N K P Z D R S P E I R P R
O H B N H A W S H R N R L E C I I Y
R O E X F L A F O U W S A C W D T Z
N P D B U S Y B E N M I C H I G A N
Q E T U L I P S P K Y Z E Z C E L D
```

A ___ driver rammed into Mr. Cadaver's car. (5)
A water ___ bit Gram. (8)
Author (6)
Ben gave one to Sal. (7)
Condition of Sal's mother's baby (9)
Don't ___ a man until you've walked two moons in his moccasins. (5)
Even though she is blind, she can see everything Phoebe is doing. (9)
Gram always wanted to see Old ___. (8)
Gram had to go there. (8)
Gram put her feet into this lake (8)
Gram's saying: _____ _____ (same word twice) (5)
He drew a picture of Sal as a lizard-like creature with long, black hair. (3)
He helped save Gram's life: ___ Fleet (3)
It skidded off the road, killing Sal's mother. (3)
It's for remembering with: peace ___ (4)
Maybe dying should be ___ and terrible, according to Ben. (6)
Mike Bickle's relationship to Mrs. Winterbottom (3)
Mrs. Partridge's son and Mrs. Cadaver's twin brother (7)
Mrs. Winterbottom leaves one for Mr. Winterbottom saying she had to go away. (4)
Name the girls give the strange boy who came to Phoebe's house (7)
One message said that everyone has his own ___. (6)
One of the whispering words Sal heard on her trip (4)
Phoebe eats dinner at this odd family's house. (7)
Phoebe thinks she murdered her husband. (7)
Phoebe's sister (8)
Place where the mysterious messages were left (5)
Police sergeant Phoebe talks to about her missing mother (6)
Sal entertained her grandparents with stories about her. (6)
Sal wanted to be in Lewiston by her mother's ___. (8)
Sal was locked in one with her grandparents for 6 days. (3)
Sal's father uncovered one when he learned Sal's mother wasn't coming home. (9)
Sal's grandparents got arrested for stealing these in Washington D.C. (5)
Sal's mother's good-bye letter says she will return before they bloom. (6)
The Black Hills are sacred to them. (5)
The Lunatic (4)
The only good thing in Pandora's box (4)
The sheriff took Sal to her mother's. (5)
The trip destination (5)
This ain't our marriage ___, but it will have to do. (3)
Walk Two ___ (5)
We had no idea all the trouble they were going to cause. (8)
Word Sal used to describe her father (6)

Walk Two Moons Word Search 2 Answer Key

A ___ driver rammed into Mr. Cadaver's car. (5)
A water ___ bit Gram. (8)
Author (6)
Ben gave one to Sal. (7)
Condition of Sal's mother's baby (9)
Don't ___ a man until you've walked two moons in his moccasins. (5)
Even though she is blind, she can see everything Phoebe is doing. (9)
Gram always wanted to see Old ___. (8)
Gram had to go there. (8)
Gram put her feet into this lake (8)
Gram's saying: _____ _____ (same word twice) (5)
He drew a picture of Sal as a lizard-like creature with long, black hair. (3)
He helped save Gram's life: ___ Fleet (3)
It skidded off the road, killing Sal's mother. (3)
It's for remembering with: peace ___ (4)
Maybe dying should be ___ and terrible, according to Ben. (6)
Mike Bickle's relationship to Mrs. Winterbottom (3)
Mrs. Partridge's son and Mrs. Cadaver's twin brother (7)
Mrs. Winterbottom leaves one for Mr. Winterbottom saying she had to go away. (4)
Name the girls give the strange boy who came to Phoebe's house (7)
One message said that everyone has his own ___. (6)
One of the whispering words Sal heard on her trip (4)
Phoebe eats dinner at this odd family's house. (7)
Phoebe thinks she murdered her husband. (7)
Phoebe's sister (8)
Place where the mysterious messages were left (5)
Police sergeant Phoebe talks to about her missing mother (6)
Sal entertained her grandparents with stories about her. (6)
Sal wanted to be in Lewiston by her mother's ___. (8)
Sal was locked in one with her grandparents for 6 days. (3)
Sal's father uncovered one when he learned Sal's mother wasn't coming home. (9)
Sal's grandparents got arrested for stealing these in Washington D.C. (5)
Sal's mother's good-bye letter says she will return before they bloom. (6)
The Black Hills are sacred to them. (5)
The Lunatic (4)
The only good thing in Pandora's box (4)
The sheriff took Sal to her mother's. (5)
The trip destination (5)
This ain't our marriage ___, but it will have to do. (3)
Walk Two ___ (5)
We had no idea all the trouble they were going to cause. (8)
Word Sal used to describe her father (6)

Walk Two Moons Word Search 3

```
Y X P W X B H J F S W P B L U N A T I C
N F X H S D P D B I X J T I M B M P W F
J O M C O W Z N N L N T R W R H D Z X P
T L R N W E F O M S W N Z L C T C J H D
P L Y M G K B T R T I G E D A C H U L W
H U Z Z A N W E T T O M M Y R B E D Z V
H Y Q B C L C F B Z F I P N S Q Z G A X
O X Z H R K M W E F C C G L L D F E G Y
P I P E E M O O N S B H D R E M I K E S
E O A C E F C P Y T N I M R A F W H N X
B S R H C I C T M I P G R W U V Z L D L
I L T C H R A I U L F A K K N N E W A D
C L R S H E S R R L A N H B W J K Y S Q
K P I O V P I E S B I K F R L A V Z I B
L K D N D L N S V O T P B U S T Y C O D
E H G F S A Q M J R H L S S D Y P Z U V
I C E V J C J C V N F V T H H Q C F X P
D A Y I P E B O M F U M D C C N R K L G
A D G F N L Z F U B L P R U D E N C E C
H A L F Y D D N H R Q D L R B J R G G L
O V M F Y J I J M M N Y Z S J Z V P Z M
K E J Z Z S T A K G C A F X H Z B V N H
K R C H I C K E N V M G L Y B M G W Q L
S A C R I F I C E S F P B S X S M B Y Z
S A L A M A N C A H O S P I T A L N N D
```

AGENDA	CHICKEN	HUZZA	MOONS	SACRIFICES
BED	CREECH	IDAHO	NORMAL	SALAMANCA
BEN	DRUNK	INDIANS	NOTE	SIMPLE
BICKLE	FAITHFUL	JOURNALS	PARTRIDGE	SIOUX
BIRKWAY	FINNEYS	JUDGE	PHOEBE	SON
BIRTHDAY	FIREPLACE	LUNATIC	PIPE	STILLBORN
BUS	GRAVE	MICHIGAN	PORCH	TIRES
CADAVER	HOPE	MIKE	PRUDENCE	TOM
CAR	HOSPITAL	MOCCASIN	RUSH	TULIPS

Walk Two Moons Word Search 3 Answer Key

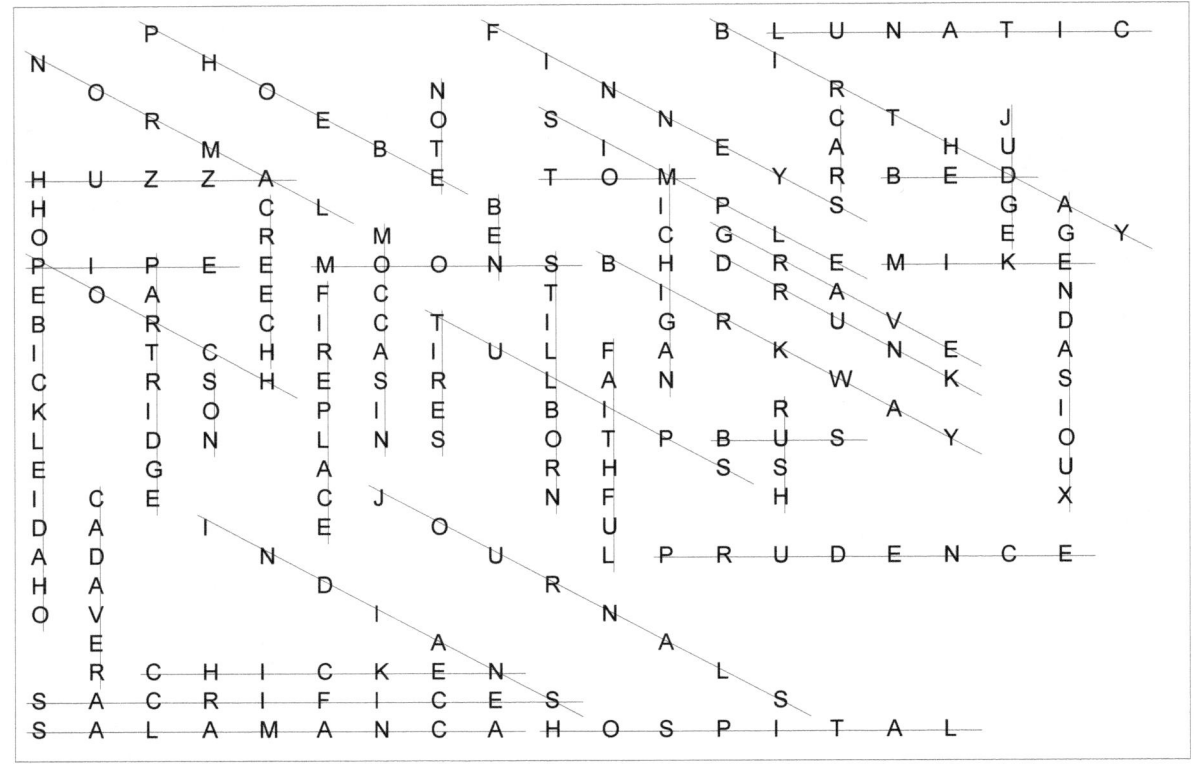

AGENDA	CHICKEN	HUZZA	MOONS	SACRIFICES
BED	CREECH	IDAHO	NORMAL	SALAMANCA
BEN	DRUNK	INDIANS	NOTE	SIMPLE
BICKLE	FAITHFUL	JOURNALS	PARTRIDGE	SIOUX
BIRKWAY	FINNEYS	JUDGE	PHOEBE	SON
BIRTHDAY	FIREPLACE	LUNATIC	PIPE	STILLBORN
BUS	GRAVE	MICHIGAN	PORCH	TIRES
CADAVER	HOPE	MIKE	PRUDENCE	TOM
CAR	HOSPITAL	MOCCASIN	RUSH	TULIPS

Walk Two Moons Word Search 4

```
T U L I P S J U D G E W G M P T Z T V C
X W F N Y T Y W T R Q Y H O D P V F F C
X P A D Y I P N X A L X P C W D C S H V
R L I I C L R F V V Z P N C J W R A J R
T J T A P L C T C E Q X W A T X B L O F
L L H N S B C F F J R T F S T T Y A U B
W W F S P O D B Z H S T Z I C H T M R B
S C U G H R W I T R Z P H N R H H A N F
C A L X G N N R F A D I M P E V B N A C
T D D G K G P T W K G P B I E V E C L W
H A H R F D H H M I K E B Q C R D A S L
Z V B F S T M D P B L M N I H H B G D B
Z E S E O F H A H O X J F D C T I U L H
C R F I N N E Y S C R Y M P A K Z G S N
V V P H M V K N H D F C J O L J L Y A F
W F K H K P W K O W N B H X O V X E C N
K T L G F S L H S T S I L C P N N F R X
P R U D E N C E P R E R U D A C S I I Y
H Y T G C Z G W I U S K N R R R B R F Y
O H N M C H B S T S I W A U T T M E I Y
E T O M N U I D A H O A T N R I H P C Q
B D R P K Z R C L T U Y I K I R J L E N
E N M D E Z T V K Y X P C Q D E J A S S
L Z A G V A H P N E L J C S G S S C T H
S Q L X V Y W R T S N Z L V E D V E X H
```

AGENDA	CHICKEN	HUZZA	MOONS	SACRIFICES
BED	CREECH	IDAHO	NORMAL	SALAMANCA
BEN	DRUNK	INDIANS	NOTE	SIMPLE
BICKLE	FAITHFUL	JOURNALS	PARTRIDGE	SIOUX
BIRKWAY	FINNEYS	JUDGE	PHOEBE	SON
BIRTHDAY	FIREPLACE	LUNATIC	PIPE	STILLBORN
BUS	GRAVE	MICHIGAN	PORCH	TIRES
CADAVER	HOPE	MIKE	PRUDENCE	TOM
CAR	HOSPITAL	MOCCASIN	RUSH	TULIPS

Walk Two Moons Word Search 4 Answer Key

AGENDA	CHICKEN	HUZZA	MOONS	SACRIFICES
BED	CREECH	IDAHO	NORMAL	SALAMANCA
BEN	DRUNK	INDIANS	NOTE	SIMPLE
BICKLE	FAITHFUL	JOURNALS	PARTRIDGE	SIOUX
BIRKWAY	FINNEYS	JUDGE	PHOEBE	SON
BIRTHDAY	FIREPLACE	LUNATIC	PIPE	STILLBORN
BUS	GRAVE	MICHIGAN	PORCH	TIRES
CADAVER	HOPE	MIKE	PRUDENCE	TOM
CAR	HOSPITAL	MOCCASIN	RUSH	TULIPS

Walk Two Moons Crossword 1

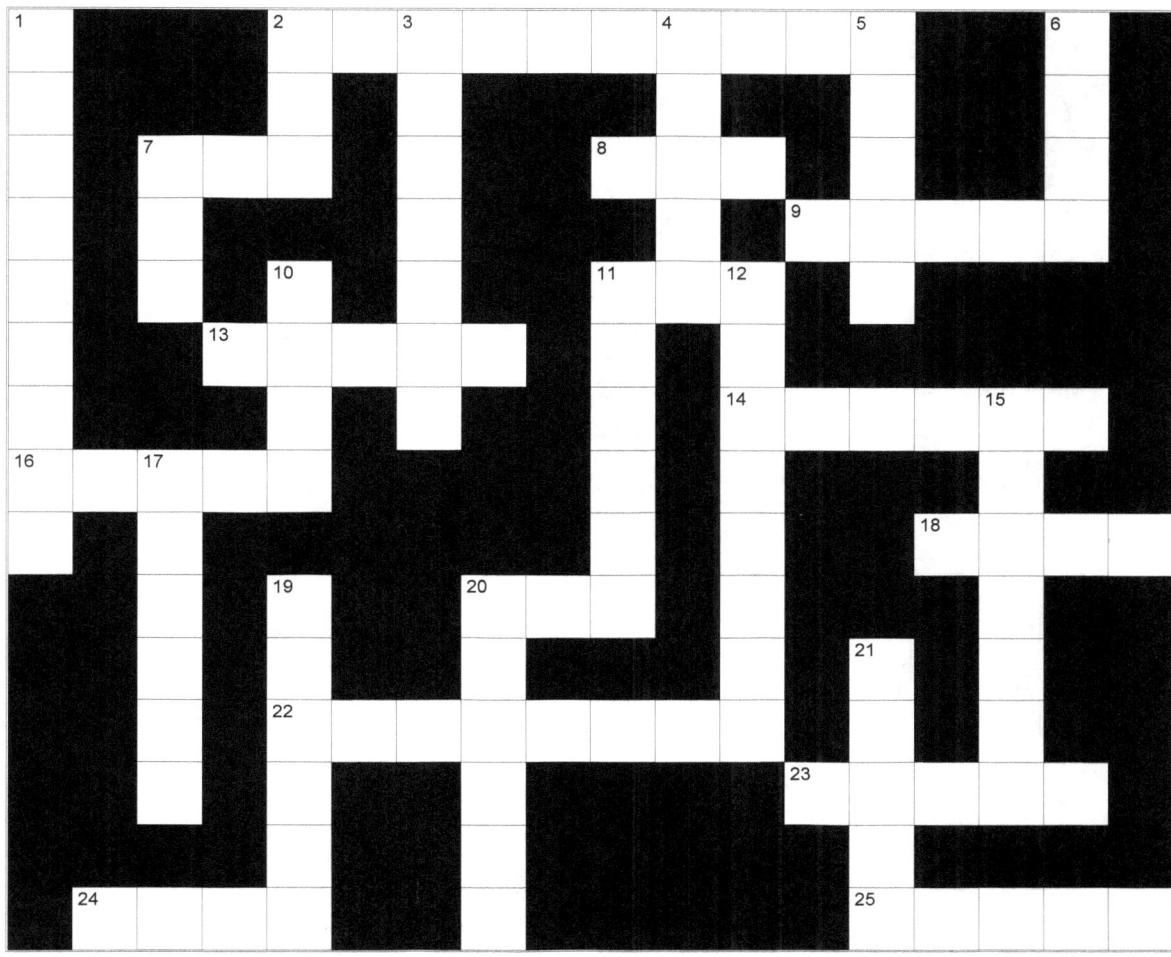

Across

2. According to Phoebe's mother, in life you have to make some ___.
7. He drew a picture of Sal as a lizard-like creature with long, black hair.
8. Sal was locked in one with her grandparents for 6 days.
9. Don't ___ a man until you've walked two moons in his moccasins.
11. He helped save Gram's life: ___ Fleet
13. Sal's grandparents got arrested for stealing these in Washington D.C.
14. Author
16. The sheriff took Sal to her mother's.
18. The Lunatic
20. It skidded off the road, killing Sal's mother.
22. A water ___ bit Gram.
23. A ___ driver rammed into Mr. Cadaver's car.
24. The only good thing in Pandora's box
25. Gram's saying: _____ _____ (same word twice)

Down

1. Even though she is blind, she can see everything Phoebe is doing.
2. Mike Bickle's relationship to Mrs. Winterbottom
3. Phoebe thinks she murdered her husband.
4. The trip destination
5. The Black Hills are sacred to them.
6. Mrs. Winterbottom leaves one for Mr. Winterbottom saying she had to go away.
7. This ain't our marriage ___, but it will have to do.
10. It's for remembering with: peace ___
11. Sal's mother's good-bye letter says she will return before they bloom.
12. Gram put her feet into this lake
15. Ben gave one to Sal.
17. One message said that everyone has his own ___.
19. Word Sal used to describe her father
20. Police sergeant Phoebe talks to about her missing mother
21. Place where the mysterious messages were left

Walk Two Moons Crossword 1 Answer Key

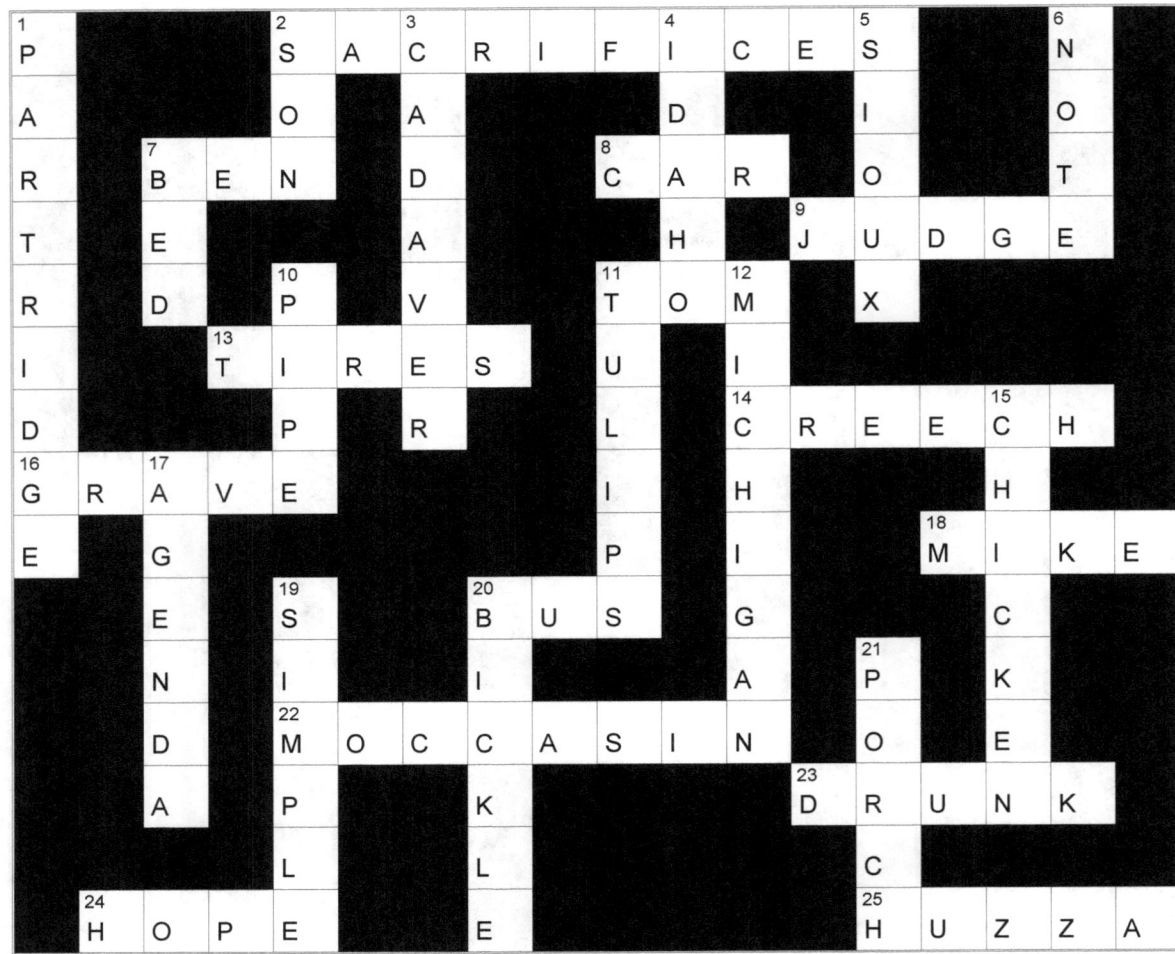

Across
2. According to Phoebe's mother, in life you have to make some ___.
7. He drew a picture of Sal as a lizard-like creature with long, black hair.
8. Sal was locked in one with her grandparents for 6 days.
9. Don't ___ a man until you've walked two moons in his moccasins.
11. He helped save Gram's life: ___ Fleet
13. Sal's grandparents got arrested for stealing these in Washington D.C.
14. Author
16. The sheriff took Sal to her mother's.
18. The Lunatic
20. It skidded off the road, killing Sal's mother.
22. A water ___ bit Gram.
23. A ___ driver rammed into Mr. Cadaver's car.
24. The only good thing in Pandora's box
25. Gram's saying: _____ _____ (same word twice)

Down
1. Even though she is blind, she can see everything Phoebe is doing.
2. Mike Bickle's relationship to Mrs. Winterbottom
3. Phoebe thinks she murdered her husband.
4. The trip destination
5. The Black Hills are sacred to them.
6. Mrs. Winterbottom leaves one for Mr. Winterbottom saying she had to go away.
7. This ain't our marriage ___, but it will have to do.
10. It's for remembering with: peace ___
11. Sal's mother's good-bye letter says she will return before they bloom.
12. Gram put her feet into this lake
15. Ben gave one to Sal.
17. One message said that everyone has his own ___.
19. Word Sal used to describe her father
20. Police sergeant Phoebe talks to about her missing mother
21. Place where the mysterious messages were left

Walk Two Moons Crossword 2

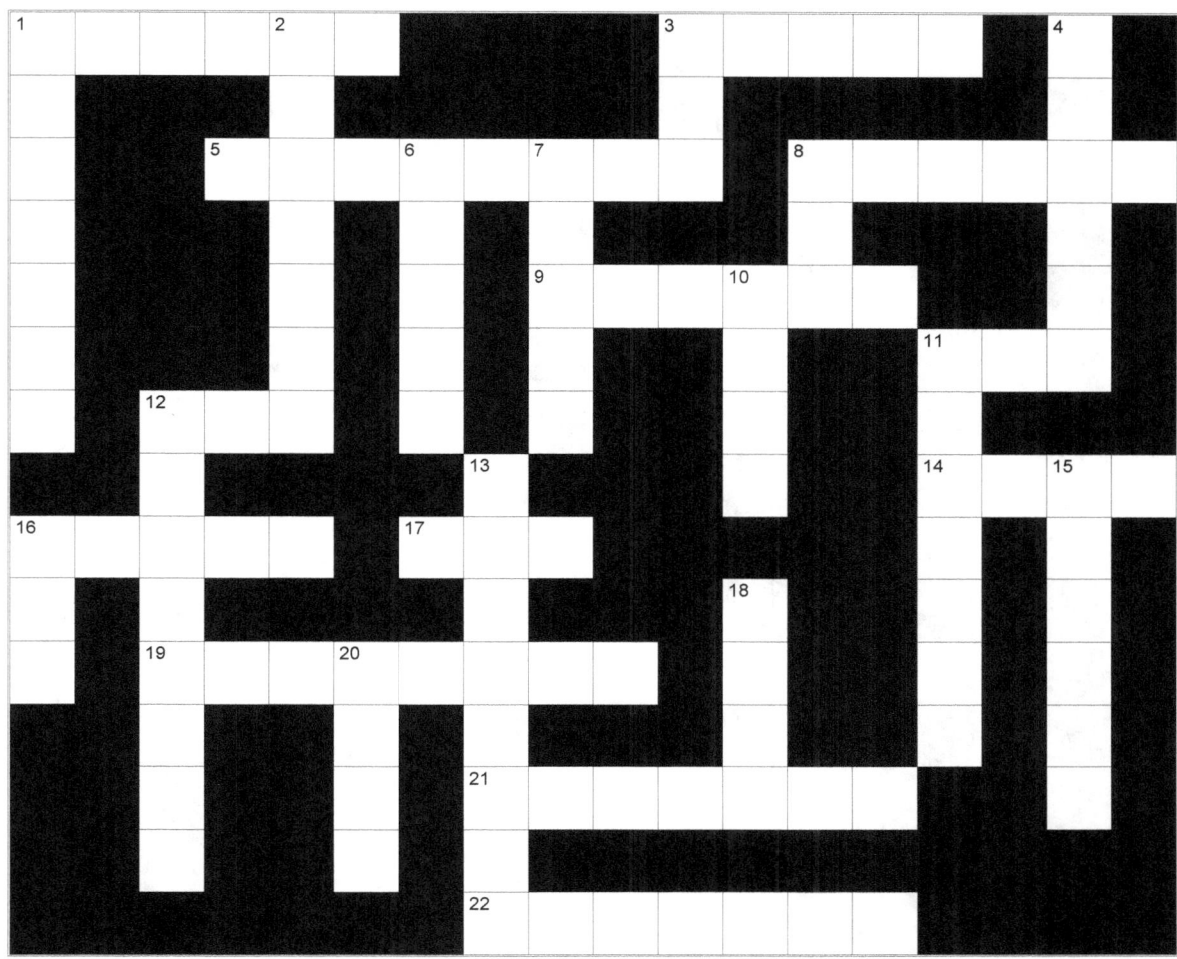

Across
1. Author
3. The Black Hills are sacred to them.
5. Gram put her feet into this lake
8. Police sergeant Phoebe talks to about her missing mother
9. One message said that everyone has his own ___.
11. It skidded off the road, killing Sal's mother.
12. He drew a picture of Sal as a lizard-like creature with long, black hair.
14. One of the whispering words Sal heard on her trip
16. Sal's grandparents got arrested for stealing these in Washington D.C.
17. Sal was locked in one with her grandparents for 6 days.
19. Gram had to go there.
21. Phoebe eats dinner at this odd family's house.
22. Name the girls give the strange boy who came to Phoebe's house

Down
1. Phoebe thinks she murdered her husband.
2. Ben gave one to Sal.
3. Mike Bickle's relationship to Mrs. Winterbottom
4. Sal's mother's good-bye letter says she will return before they bloom.
6. Gram's saying: _____ _____ (same word twice)
7. The sheriff took Sal to her mother's.
8. This ain't our marriage ___, but it will have to do.
10. Mrs. Winterbottom leaves one for Mr. Winterbottom saying she had to go away.
11. Mrs. Partridge's son and Mrs. Cadaver's twin brother
12. Sal wanted to be in Lewiston by her mother's ___.
13. Gram always wanted to see Old ___.
15. Word Sal used to describe her father
16. He helped save Gram's life: ___ Fleet
18. The Lunatic
20. It's for remembering with: peace ___

Walk Two Moons Crossword 2 Answer Key

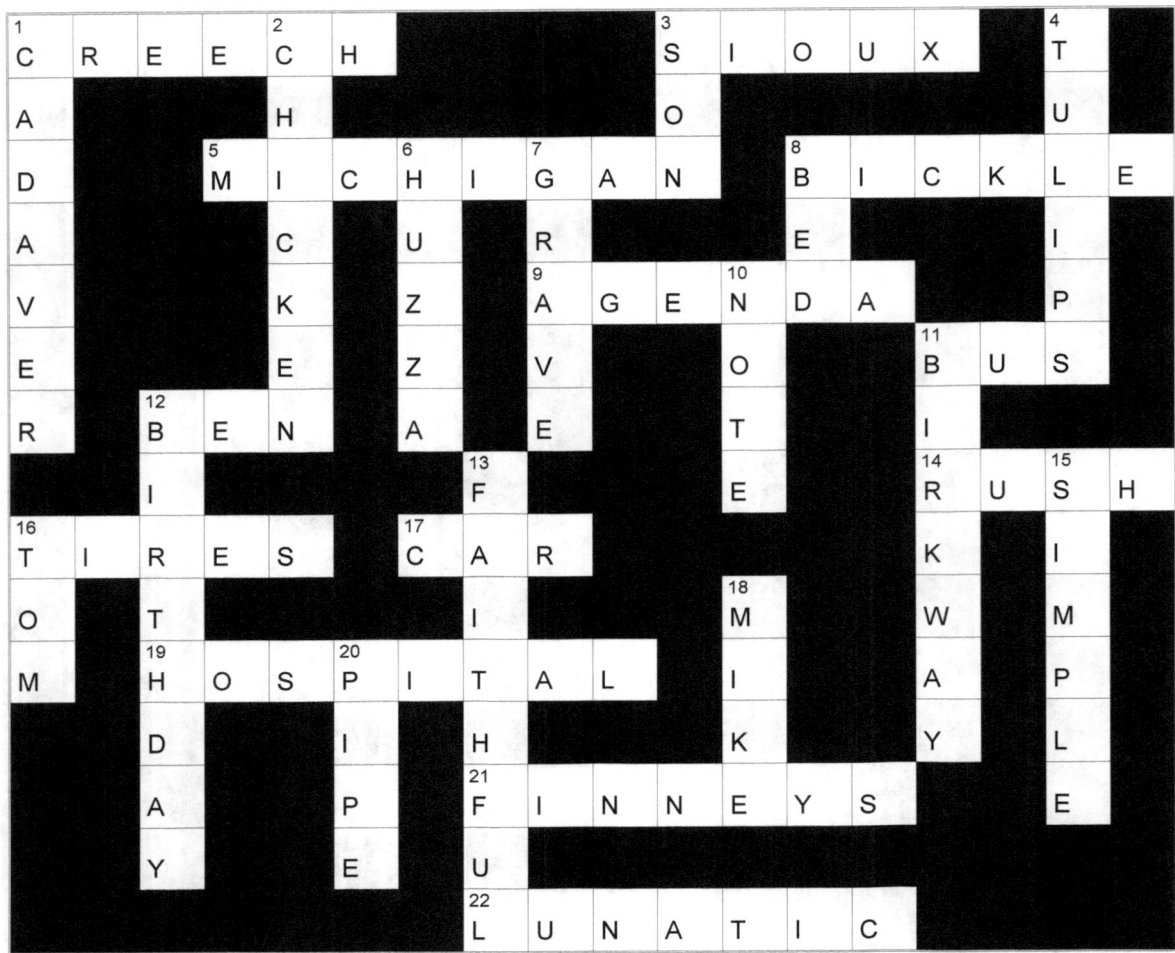

Across
1. Author
3. The Black Hills are sacred to them.
5. Gram put her feet into this lake
8. Police sergeant Phoebe talks to about her missing mother
9. One message said that everyone has his own ___.
11. It skidded off the road, killing Sal's mother.
12. He drew a picture of Sal as a lizard-like creature with long, black hair.
14. One of the whispering words Sal heard on her trip
16. Sal's grandparents got arrested for stealing these in Washington D.C.
17. Sal was locked in one with her grandparents for 6 days.
19. Gram had to go there.
21. Phoebe eats dinner at this odd family's house.
22. Name the girls give the strange boy who came to Phoebe's house

Down
1. Phoebe thinks she murdered her husband.
2. Ben gave one to Sal.
3. Mike Bickle's relationship to Mrs. Winterbottom
4. Sal's mother's good-bye letter says she will return before they bloom.
6. Gram's saying: _____ _____ (same word twice)
7. The sheriff took Sal to her mother's.
8. This ain't our marriage ___, but it will have to do.
10. Mrs. Winterbottom leaves one for Mr. Winterbottom saying she had to go away.
11. Mrs. Partridge's son and Mrs. Cadaver's twin brother
12. Sal wanted to be in Lewiston by her mother's ___.
13. Gram always wanted to see Old ___.
15. Word Sal used to describe her father
16. He helped save Gram's life: ___ Fleet
18. The Lunatic
20. It's for remembering with: peace ___

Walk Two Moons Crossword 3

Across

1. The only good thing in Pandora's box
3. Don't ___ a man until you've walked two moons in his moccasins.
8. Sal entertained her grandparents with stories about her.
10. One message said that everyone has his own ___.
11. Sal was locked in one with her grandparents for 6 days.
12. Mrs. Winterbottom leaves one for Mr. Winterbottom saying she had to go away.
14. The trip destination
15. The Lunatic
16. Phoebe eats dinner at this odd family's house.
19. It's for remembering with: peace ___
21. The Black Hills are sacred to them.
23. One of the whispering words Sal heard on her trip
24. Sal's father uncovered one when he learned Sal's mother wasn't coming home.
25. Author

Down

1. Gram had to go there.
2. Place where the mysterious messages were left
4. The sheriff took Sal to her mother's.
5. Phoebe thinks she murdered her husband.
6. He helped save Gram's life: ___ Fleet
7. This ain't our marriage ___, but it will have to do.
8. Phoebe's sister
9. He drew a picture of Sal as a lizard-like creature with long, black hair.
13. Sal's grandparents got arrested for stealing these in Washington D.C.
15. Walk Two ___
16. Gram always wanted to see Old ___.
17. Mike Bickle's relationship to Mrs. Winterbottom
18. Maybe dying should be ___ and terrible, according to Ben.
20. Word Sal used to describe her father
22. A ___ driver rammed into Mr. Cadaver's car.

Walk Two Moons Crossword 3 Answer Key

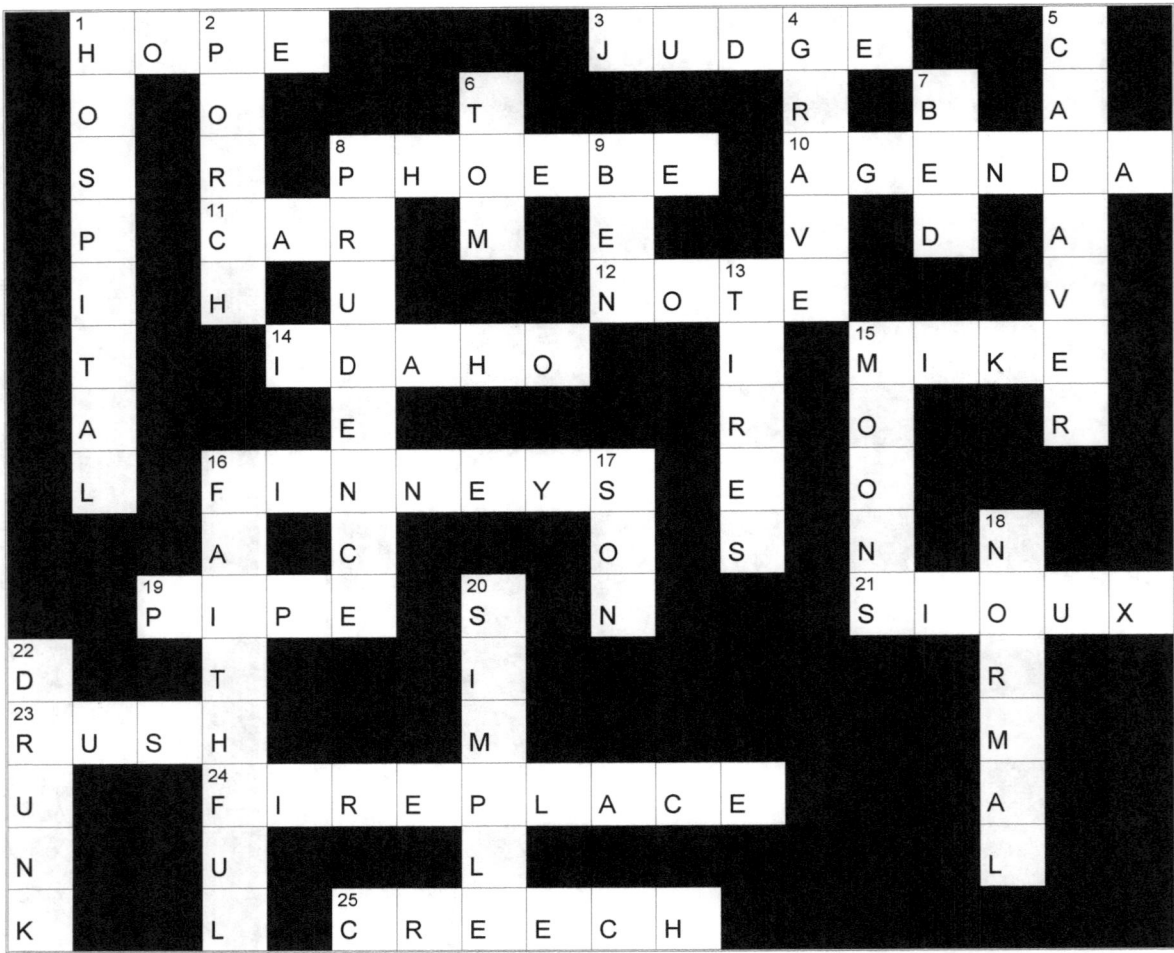

Across
1. The only good thing in Pandora's box
3. Don't ___ a man until you've walked two moons in his moccasins.
8. Sal entertained her grandparents with stories about her.
10. One message said that everyone has his own ___.
11. Sal was locked in one with her grandparents for 6 days.
12. Mrs. Winterbottom leaves one for Mr. Winterbottom saying she had to go away.
14. The trip destination
15. The Lunatic
16. Phoebe eats dinner at this odd family's house.
19. It's for remembering with: peace ___
21. The Black Hills are sacred to them.
23. One of the whispering words Sal heard on her trip
24. Sal's father uncovered one when he learned Sal's mother wasn't coming home.
25. Author

Down
1. Gram had to go there.
2. Place where the mysterious messages were left
4. The sheriff took Sal to her mother's.
5. Phoebe thinks she murdered her husband.
6. He helped save Gram's life: ___ Fleet
7. This ain't our marriage ___, but it will have to do.
8. Phoebe's sister
9. He drew a picture of Sal as a lizard-like creature with long, black hair.
13. Sal's grandparents got arrested for stealing these in Washington D.C.
15. Walk Two ___
16. Gram always wanted to see Old ___.
17. Mike Bickle's relationship to Mrs. Winterbottom
18. Maybe dying should be ___ and terrible, according to Ben.
20. Word Sal used to describe her father
22. A ___ driver rammed into Mr. Cadaver's car.

Walk Two Moons Crossword 4

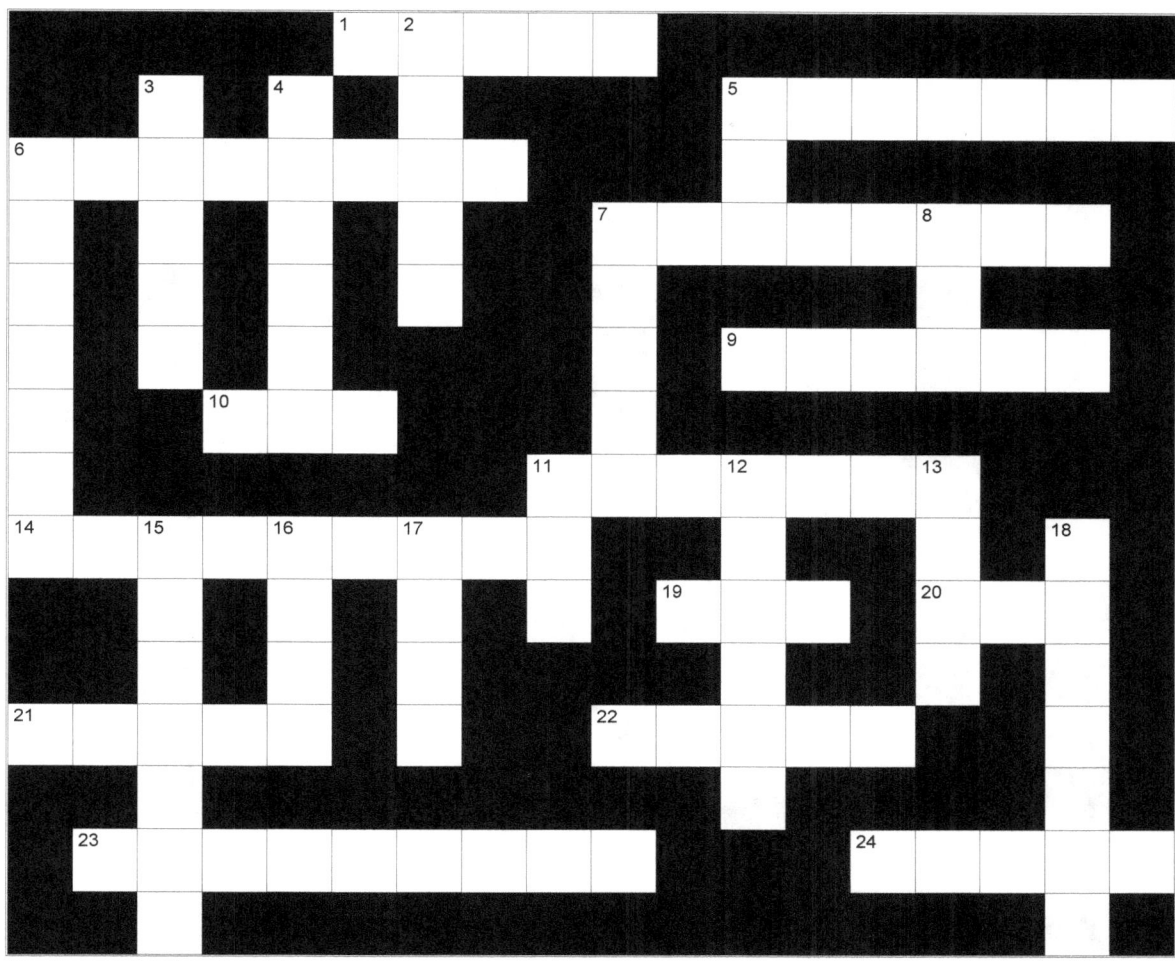

Across

1. The trip destination
5. Mrs. Partridge's son and Mrs. Cadaver's twin brother
6. Gram always wanted to see Old ___.
7. Gram had to go there.
9. Maybe dying should be ___ and terrible, according to Ben.
10. He drew a picture of Sal as a lizard-like creature with long, black hair.
11. Phoebe thinks she murdered her husband.
14. Sal's whole first name
19. This ain't our marriage ___, but it will have to do.
20. Mike Bickle's relationship to Mrs. Winterbottom
21. The sheriff took Sal to her mother's.
22. Don't ___ a man until you've walked two moons in his moccasins.
23. Sal's father uncovered one when he learned Sal's mother wasn't coming home.
24. Walk Two ___

Down

2. A ___ driver rammed into Mr. Cadaver's car.
3. Sal's grandparents got arrested for stealing these in Washington D.C.
4. Sal entertained her grandparents with stories about her.
5. It skidded off the road, killing Sal's mother.
6. Phoebe eats dinner at this odd family's house.
7. Gram's saying: _____ _____ (same word twice)
8. He helped save Gram's life: ___ Fleet
11. Sal was locked in one with her grandparents for 6 days.
12. One message said that everyone has his own ___.
13. One of the whispering words Sal heard on her trip
15. Name the girls give the strange boy who came to Phoebe's house
16. The Lunatic
17. Mrs. Winterbottom leaves one for Mr. Winterbottom saying she had to go away.
18. Gram dances with them.

Walk Two Moons Crossword 4 Answer Key

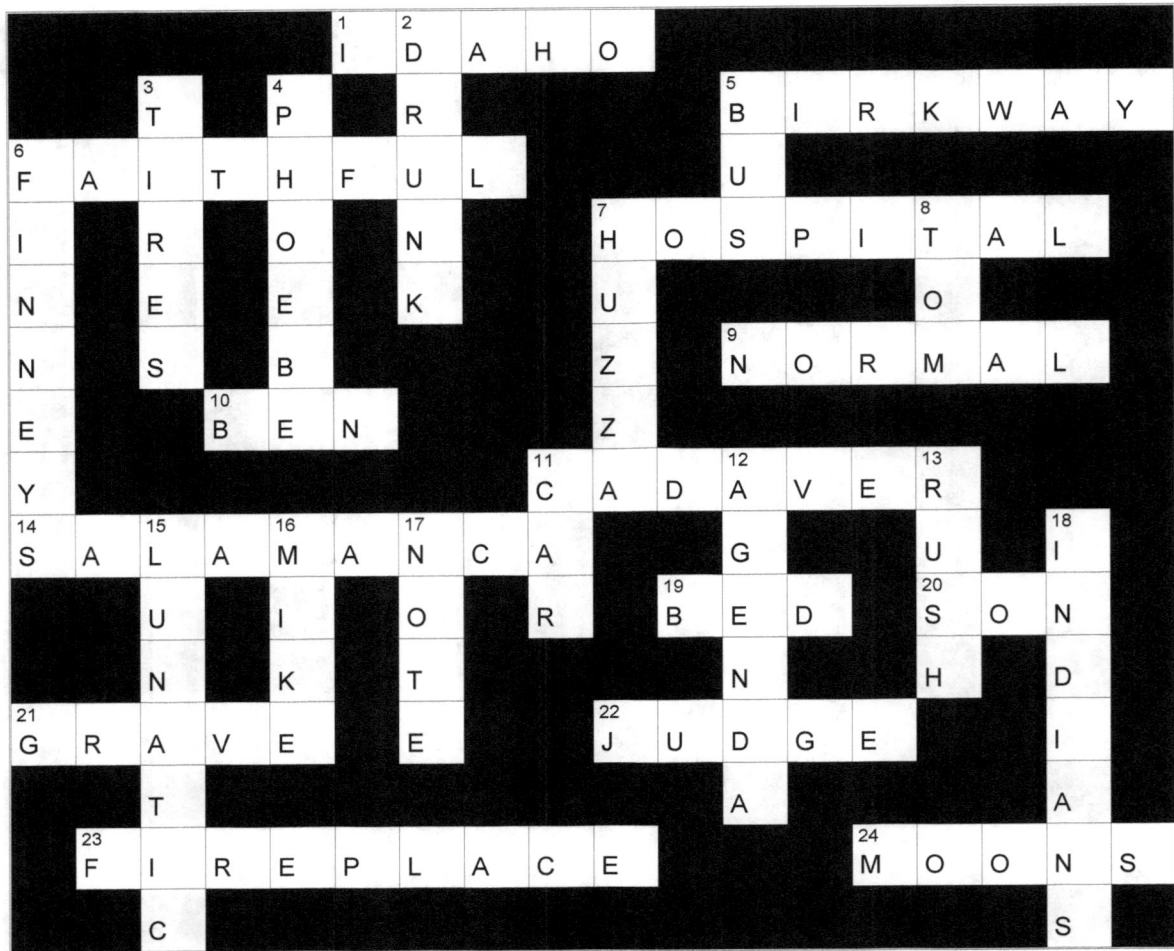

Across
1. The trip destination
5. Mrs. Partridge's son and Mrs. Cadaver's twin brother
6. Gram always wanted to see Old ___.
7. Gram had to go there.
9. Maybe dying should be ___ and terrible, according to Ben.
10. He drew a picture of Sal as a lizard-like creature with long, black hair.
11. Phoebe thinks she murdered her husband.
14. Sal's whole first name
19. This ain't our marriage ___, but it will have to do.
20. Mike Bickle's relationship to Mrs. Winterbottom
21. The sheriff took Sal to her mother's.
22. Don't ___ a man until you've walked two moons in his moccasins.
23. Sal's father uncovered one when he learned Sal's mother wasn't coming home.
24. Walk Two ___

Down
2. A ___ driver rammed into Mr. Cadaver's car.
3. Sal's grandparents got arrested for stealing these in Washington D.C.
4. Sal entertained her grandparents with stories about her.
5. It skidded off the road, killing Sal's mother.
6. Phoebe eats dinner at this odd family's house.
7. Gram's saying: _____ _____ (same word twice)
8. He helped save Gram's life: ___ Fleet
11. Sal was locked in one with her grandparents for 6 days.
12. One message said that everyone has his own ___.
13. One of the whispering words Sal heard on her trip
15. Name the girls give the strange boy who came to Phoebe's house
16. The Lunatic
17. Mrs. Winterbottom leaves one for Mr. Winterbottom saying she had to go away.
18. Gram dances with them.

Walk Two Moons

TOM	PORCH	FINNEYS	PARTRIDGE	CADAVER
BICKLE	BUS	JOURNALS	STILLBORN	HOPE
CHICKEN	SALAMANCA	FREE SPACE	PIPE	BIRTHDAY
RUSH	PHOEBE	BIRKWAY	SIOUX	TIRES
MOCCASIN	TULIPS	CREECH	GRAVE	MOONS

Walk Two Moons

MIKE	PRUDENCE	NORMAL	CAR	HOSPITAL
SACRIFICES	INDIANS	BEN	JUDGE	SIMPLE
AGENDA	MICHIGAN	FREE SPACE	FIREPLACE	DRUNK
LUNATIC	IDAHO	HUZZA	BED	SON
MOONS	GRAVE	CREECH	TULIPS	MOCCASIN

Walk Two Moons

PHOEBE	JOURNALS	BUS	SON	MOCCASIN
BIRKWAY	DRUNK	BED	PIPE	BEN
MOONS	CHICKEN	FREE SPACE	PARTRIDGE	SALAMANCA
NORMAL	HUZZA	STILLBORN	TOM	RUSH
FAITHFUL	JUDGE	HOSPITAL	GRAVE	INDIANS

Walk Two Moons

MICHIGAN	BIRTHDAY	FIREPLACE	SIOUX	CAR
TULIPS	FINNEYS	IDAHO	PORCH	CADAVER
MIKE	SACRIFICES	FREE SPACE	SIMPLE	AGENDA
BICKLE	TIRES	NOTE	HOPE	PRUDENCE
INDIANS	GRAVE	HOSPITAL	JUDGE	FAITHFUL

Walk Two Moons

TOM	SALAMANCA	TULIPS	CHICKEN	FIREPLACE
HUZZA	SIOUX	STILLBORN	BUS	SON
NOTE	SIMPLE	FREE SPACE	GRAVE	JUDGE
PARTRIDGE	MICHIGAN	PHOEBE	BIRKWAY	CAR
PIPE	NORMAL	SACRIFICES	CADAVER	MOONS

Walk Two Moons

JOURNALS	DRUNK	FINNEYS	MIKE	INDIANS
PRUDENCE	PORCH	LUNATIC	CREECH	HOPE
BEN	TIRES	FREE SPACE	RUSH	BED
BICKLE	HOSPITAL	MOCCASIN	IDAHO	BIRTHDAY
MOONS	CADAVER	SACRIFICES	NORMAL	PIPE

Walk Two Moons

BICKLE	TOM	TULIPS	PHOEBE	BUS
BIRTHDAY	HOPE	CAR	CREECH	STILLBORN
SIMPLE	SACRIFICES	FREE SPACE	MIKE	CADAVER
JUDGE	INDIANS	CHICKEN	LUNATIC	MOONS
HOSPITAL	GRAVE	BIRKWAY	PRUDENCE	MICHIGAN

Walk Two Moons

BEN	SALAMANCA	FINNEYS	HUZZA	RUSH
MOCCASIN	NOTE	NORMAL	PORCH	AGENDA
TIRES	PIPE	FREE SPACE	JOURNALS	SON
FIREPLACE	SIOUX	BED	FAITHFUL	PARTRIDGE
MICHIGAN	PRUDENCE	BIRKWAY	GRAVE	HOSPITAL

Walk Two Moons

MOONS	PORCH	CADAVER	CHICKEN	IDAHO
SACRIFICES	FIREPLACE	TIRES	BIRKWAY	NORMAL
SIOUX	FINNEYS	FREE SPACE	PIPE	MOCCASIN
CREECH	RUSH	JUDGE	AGENDA	CAR
TULIPS	HOPE	TOM	STILLBORN	NOTE

Walk Two Moons

HOSPITAL	PARTRIDGE	HUZZA	INDIANS	BUS
DRUNK	FAITHFUL	PHOEBE	SIMPLE	BIRTHDAY
BEN	LUNATIC	FREE SPACE	JOURNALS	BICKLE
GRAVE	MICHIGAN	MIKE	BED	PRUDENCE
NOTE	STILLBORN	TOM	HOPE	TULIPS

Walk Two Moons

GRAVE	MICHIGAN	TIRES	PHOEBE	TULIPS
HOSPITAL	MOONS	SIOUX	FAITHFUL	LUNATIC
MIKE	BIRTHDAY	FREE SPACE	SON	CAR
BEN	FIREPLACE	CREECH	MOCCASIN	AGENDA
NORMAL	HOPE	PORCH	NOTE	SIMPLE

Walk Two Moons

BIRKWAY	JUDGE	BED	INDIANS	JOURNALS
STILLBORN	RUSH	BUS	SALAMANCA	SACRIFICES
IDAHO	PIPE	FREE SPACE	HUZZA	DRUNK
TOM	CADAVER	PARTRIDGE	FINNEYS	PRUDENCE
SIMPLE	NOTE	PORCH	HOPE	NORMAL

Walk Two Moons

PARTRIDGE	MIKE	LUNATIC	TOM	RUSH
FIREPLACE	BED	SIMPLE	TIRES	NOTE
MOCCASIN	BIRTHDAY	FREE SPACE	STILLBORN	IDAHO
PORCH	PIPE	HOPE	CHICKEN	BUS
SIOUX	TULIPS	HOSPITAL	SACRIFICES	JOURNALS

Walk Two Moons

BICKLE	SALAMANCA	PRUDENCE	MICHIGAN	CAR
CREECH	PHOEBE	AGENDA	MOONS	HUZZA
FAITHFUL	DRUNK	FREE SPACE	BEN	JUDGE
BIRKWAY	CADAVER	SON	NORMAL	FINNEYS
JOURNALS	SACRIFICES	HOSPITAL	TULIPS	SIOUX

Walk Two Moons

SACRIFICES	JOURNALS	NORMAL	HOSPITAL	CHICKEN
FIREPLACE	SIOUX	BEN	PHOEBE	CAR
SIMPLE	BED	FREE SPACE	BIRTHDAY	BIRKWAY
SON	BICKLE	HUZZA	PARTRIDGE	FAITHFUL
PIPE	GRAVE	INDIANS	TIRES	MIKE

Walk Two Moons

MICHIGAN	TULIPS	TOM	DRUNK	RUSH
PRUDENCE	NOTE	MOCCASIN	STILLBORN	PORCH
CREECH	IDAHO	FREE SPACE	BUS	LUNATIC
MOONS	HOPE	FINNEYS	SALAMANCA	CADAVER
MIKE	TIRES	INDIANS	GRAVE	PIPE

Walk Two Moons

BED	FINNEYS	SIOUX	HOPE	BUS
JUDGE	PORCH	HOSPITAL	NORMAL	BIRTHDAY
SALAMANCA	MIKE	FREE SPACE	TIRES	FIREPLACE
CHICKEN	HUZZA	MOONS	TOM	MICHIGAN
TULIPS	SACRIFICES	RUSH	PARTRIDGE	PHOEBE

Walk Two Moons

CAR	MOCCASIN	NOTE	SIMPLE	BIRKWAY
GRAVE	JOURNALS	DRUNK	AGENDA	SON
CREECH	BEN	FREE SPACE	INDIANS	FAITHFUL
STILLBORN	BICKLE	PRUDENCE	PIPE	IDAHO
PHOEBE	PARTRIDGE	RUSH	SACRIFICES	TULIPS

Walk Two Moons

SIOUX	PHOEBE	INDIANS	PARTRIDGE	STILLBORN
MOCCASIN	BICKLE	CREECH	FIREPLACE	PRUDENCE
BIRTHDAY	IDAHO	FREE SPACE	BED	FAITHFUL
TIRES	BIRKWAY	MOONS	MIKE	CAR
BUS	BEN	DRUNK	SALAMANCA	FINNEYS

Walk Two Moons

JOURNALS	MICHIGAN	SON	CADAVER	LUNATIC
CHICKEN	TULIPS	NORMAL	SIMPLE	HOSPITAL
NOTE	TOM	FREE SPACE	SACRIFICES	PORCH
HOPE	AGENDA	PIPE	RUSH	JUDGE
FINNEYS	SALAMANCA	DRUNK	BEN	BUS

Walk Two Moons

FINNEYS	HOPE	SIMPLE	SIOUX	BICKLE
FAITHFUL	IDAHO	HOSPITAL	MIKE	TULIPS
DRUNK	CHICKEN	FREE SPACE	RUSH	INDIANS
SALAMANCA	TIRES	PARTRIDGE	PHOEBE	SACRIFICES
MOONS	CAR	STILLBORN	GRAVE	PIPE

Walk Two Moons

NOTE	NORMAL	BIRTHDAY	BIRKWAY	PORCH
BED	TOM	CREECH	LUNATIC	PRUDENCE
MICHIGAN	AGENDA	FREE SPACE	CADAVER	FIREPLACE
BUS	HUZZA	BEN	MOCCASIN	JUDGE
PIPE	GRAVE	STILLBORN	CAR	MOONS

Walk Two Moons

JUDGE	STILLBORN	BIRKWAY	MOCCASIN	MICHIGAN
SIOUX	BIRTHDAY	TOM	LUNATIC	HOSPITAL
DRUNK	SACRIFICES	FREE SPACE	CADAVER	IDAHO
TULIPS	TIRES	JOURNALS	HUZZA	FAITHFUL
MIKE	MOONS	NOTE	SIMPLE	INDIANS

Walk Two Moons

CAR	BED	PRUDENCE	NORMAL	AGENDA
BUS	PORCH	BICKLE	RUSH	PIPE
FINNEYS	PARTRIDGE	FREE SPACE	GRAVE	BEN
SON	CHICKEN	FIREPLACE	CREECH	PHOEBE
INDIANS	SIMPLE	NOTE	MOONS	MIKE

Walk Two Moons

TIRES	SALAMANCA	SON	BICKLE	NORMAL
FIREPLACE	STILLBORN	AGENDA	CAR	JUDGE
SIMPLE	TULIPS	FREE SPACE	FAITHFUL	PORCH
SIOUX	PIPE	NOTE	MIKE	CREECH
DRUNK	INDIANS	FINNEYS	RUSH	HOSPITAL

Walk Two Moons

JOURNALS	SACRIFICES	TOM	PARTRIDGE	BUS
BIRTHDAY	PRUDENCE	MOONS	HUZZA	HOPE
BEN	PHOEBE	FREE SPACE	IDAHO	CHICKEN
BIRKWAY	LUNATIC	GRAVE	MICHIGAN	BED
HOSPITAL	RUSH	FINNEYS	INDIANS	DRUNK

Walk Two Moons

CAR	BIRKWAY	PHOEBE	MIKE	IDAHO
PORCH	BICKLE	FINNEYS	LUNATIC	SIMPLE
MOONS	BED	FREE SPACE	PRUDENCE	NOTE
STILLBORN	TULIPS	HOPE	HOSPITAL	MOCCASIN
SACRIFICES	CHICKEN	INDIANS	SALAMANCA	BUS

Walk Two Moons

TIRES	RUSH	FIREPLACE	NORMAL	SIOUX
PIPE	HUZZA	BIRTHDAY	CREECH	DRUNK
PARTRIDGE	GRAVE	FREE SPACE	JOURNALS	CADAVER
SON	JUDGE	TOM	AGENDA	MICHIGAN
BUS	SALAMANCA	INDIANS	CHICKEN	SACRIFICES

Walk Two Moons

FINNEYS	CREECH	DRUNK	SON	BIRKWAY
CADAVER	JUDGE	RUSH	SACRIFICES	FAITHFUL
PARTRIDGE	TIRES	FREE SPACE	CAR	PRUDENCE
TULIPS	PHOEBE	BEN	NOTE	HOPE
GRAVE	HUZZA	MOONS	MIKE	STILLBORN

Walk Two Moons

JOURNALS	SIMPLE	IDAHO	PIPE	TOM
SIOUX	BIRTHDAY	BICKLE	FIREPLACE	LUNATIC
PORCH	CHICKEN	FREE SPACE	MICHIGAN	BED
AGENDA	INDIANS	NORMAL	HOSPITAL	MOCCASIN
STILLBORN	MIKE	MOONS	HUZZA	GRAVE

Walk Two Moons

DRUNK	MICHIGAN	HOSPITAL	PORCH	PHOEBE
SIMPLE	BIRTHDAY	FIREPLACE	TIRES	CAR
JUDGE	GRAVE	FREE SPACE	LUNATIC	HUZZA
RUSH	NORMAL	MOCCASIN	SIOUX	CADAVER
BIRKWAY	INDIANS	PARTRIDGE	IDAHO	TULIPS

Walk Two Moons

JOURNALS	BUS	BED	BICKLE	STILLBORN
CREECH	CHICKEN	PRUDENCE	SALAMANCA	NOTE
MIKE	AGENDA	FREE SPACE	TOM	MOONS
PIPE	BEN	HOPE	SON	FAITHFUL
TULIPS	IDAHO	PARTRIDGE	INDIANS	BIRKWAY

Walk Two Moons Vocabulary Word List

No.	Word	Clue/Definition
1.	ACCUMULATED	Collected or gathered together
2.	AMBUSH	Surprise attack from hidden assailants
3.	AMNESIA	Partial or total loss of memory caused by brain injury or shock
4.	ANONYMOUS	Given or written by a person whose name is unknown
5.	BADGERED	Pestered
6.	BERSERK	In a state of violent or destructive rage or frenzy
7.	BESIEGING	Harassing
8.	BETRAYED	Deceived
9.	BOUNTIFUL	Plentiful
10.	CABOODLE	Lot; group
11.	CADAVER	Dead body
12.	CANTANKEROUS	Quarrelsome
13.	CAPTIVE	One taken or held prisoner
14.	CAVORTED	Pranced
15.	CHISEL	Hand tool with a sharp, wedged blade
16.	CHOLESTEROL	White sterol found in animal fats. Excessive amounts can cause blocked arteries.
17.	COLOSSAL	Huge; gigantic
18.	CONSOLE	Comfort
19.	CRUCIAL	Of supreme importance
20.	DEFENSIVE	Feeling under attack and hence quick to justify one's actions
21.	DEFIANCE	Bold resistance to authority
22.	DEFYING	Challenging; daring
23.	DEPRIVED	To have undergone a loss; to not have something
24.	DESPAIRING	Giving up hope
25.	DIABOLIC	Very wicked or cruel
26.	DISSUADE	Persuade against (an action)
27.	ELABORATE	Add more details
28.	EMBEDDED	Set or fixed firmly
29.	EXTENSIVELY	To a great degree
30.	FIENDS	Persons addicted to some activity or habit
31.	FRAGILE	Physically weak; delicate
32.	GHASTLY	Horrible; frightful
33.	GNARLED	Knotty & twisted, as in the trunk of an old tree
34.	GORGES	Deep narrow passes between steep heights
35.	HAIRPIN	U-shaped
36.	HANKERING	Craving; yearning
37.	HOLSTER	Pistol holder
38.	HORRID	Causing a feeling of horror; ugly; unpleasant
39.	HYPNOTIZED	Put into a trance-like condition
40.	IMPULSE	An impelling force, usually from within
41.	INTRIGUING	Exciting interest of curiosity
42.	LEGITIMATE	Legal; proper; within the law
43.	MALEVOLENT	Wishing evil or harm to others
44.	MALINGER	Pretend to be ill to escape work
45.	MANNA	Divine aids; spiritual sustenance
46.	MIGRAINE	Intense, periodically returning headache
47.	MISCELLANEOUS	Varied; mixed
48.	MOCCASINS	Soft, heelless, leather slippers originally worn by North American Indians
49.	MOURNFULLY	Sadly

Walk Two Moons Vocabulary Word List (continued)

No.	Word	Clue/Definition
50.	MUESLI	Breakfast cereal like granola
51.	NOBLE	Showing high moral qualities
52.	OMNIPOTENT	Having unlimited power
53.	OPTIMISTIC	Having the tendency to expect the best outcome
54.	ORNERY	Mischievous
55.	PANDEMONIUM	Wild disorder, noise, or confusion
56.	PANDORA	In Greek mythology, the first mortal woman; out o curiosity she opens a box
57.	PERCOLATING	Bubbling up
58.	PIOUS	Having or showing religious devotion
59.	PLAGUES	Epidemic diseases that are deadly
60.	PREJUDGMENTS	Judgments without all the evidence
61.	PROMETHEUS	Titan in Greek mythology who steals fire from heaven for the benefit of mankind
62.	RASPY	Grating; easily irritated; rough
63.	REASSURANCE	Restored confidence
64.	RELUCTANT	Unwilling; hesitant
65.	RHODODENDRON	Shrub with showy flowers of pink, white, or purple
66.	RUINATION	Demise, destruction or decay
67.	RUMMAGING	Searching thoroughly by moving the contents about
68.	SKEPTICAL	Not easily convinced or persuaded; doubtful
69.	SPARE	Refrain from troubling or worrying
70.	SPIRE	Top of a pointed, tapering object or structure, as a mountain peak
71.	STILLBORN	Dead when delivered from the womb
72.	SULLEN	Gloomy; dismal
73.	TENTATIVELY	Hesitantly
74.	TREACHEROUS	Dangerously unstable
75.	UNADULTERATED	Pure
76.	WEANING	Adapting a young child or animal to go without something

Walk Two Moons Vocabulary Fill in the Blanks 1

_____ 1. An impelling force, usually from within

_____ 2. Searching thoroughly by moving the contents about

_____ 3. Sadly

_____ 4. Intense, periodically returning headache

_____ 5. Top of a pointed, tapering object or structure, as a mountain peak

_____ 6. Having or showing religious devotion

_____ 7. Lot; group

_____ 8. Demise, destruction or decay

_____ 9. Harassing

_____ 10. Deceived

_____ 11. Mischievous

_____ 12. Legal; proper; within the law

_____ 13. Restored confidence

_____ 14. Dead body

_____ 15. Plentiful

_____ 16. White sterol found in animal fats. Excessive amounts can cause blocked arteries.

_____ 17. Physically weak; delicate

_____ 18. Pure

_____ 19. Dangerously unstable

_____ 20. Unwilling; hesitant

Walk Two Moons Vocabulary Fill in the Blanks 1 Answer Key

IMPULSE	1. An impelling force, usually from within
RUMMAGING	2. Searching thoroughly by moving the contents about
MOURNFULLY	3. Sadly
MIGRAINE	4. Intense, periodically returning headache
SPIRE	5. Top of a pointed, tapering object or structure, as a mountain peak
PIOUS	6. Having or showing religious devotion
CABOODLE	7. Lot; group
RUINATION	8. Demise, destruction or decay
BESIEGING	9. Harassing
BETRAYED	10. Deceived
ORNERY	11. Mischievous
LEGITIMATE	12. Legal; proper; within the law
REASSURANCE	13. Restored confidence
CADAVER	14. Dead body
BOUNTIFUL	15. Plentiful
CHOLESTEROL	16. White sterol found in animal fats. Excessive amounts can cause blocked arteries.
FRAGILE	17. Physically weak; delicate
UNADULTERATED	18. Pure
TREACHEROUS	19. Dangerously unstable
RELUCTANT	20. Unwilling; hesitant

Walk Two Moons Vocabulary Fill in the Blanks 2

_____ 1. Bold resistance to authority

_____ 2. Pistol holder

_____ 3. Deep narrow passes between steep heights

_____ 4. Restored confidence

_____ 5. Persuade against (an action)

_____ 6. Pure

_____ 7. Dead when delivered from the womb

_____ 8. Mischievous

_____ 9. Titan in Greek mythology who steals fire from heaven for the benefit of mankind

_____ 10. In a state of violent or destructive rage or frenzy

_____ 11. Top of a pointed, tapering object or structure, as a mountain peak

_____ 12. Intense, periodically returning headache

_____ 13. Craving; yearning

_____ 14. Surprise attack from hidden assailants

_____ 15. Giving up hope

_____ 16. Dangerously unstable

_____ 17. Having the tendency to expect the best outcome

_____ 18. Comfort

_____ 19. Pranced

_____ 20. Not easily convinced or persuaded; doubtful

Walk Two Moons Vocabulary Fill in the Blanks 2 Answer Key

DEFIANCE	1. Bold resistance to authority
HOLSTER	2. Pistol holder
GORGES	3. Deep narrow passes between steep heights
REASSURANCE	4. Restored confidence
DISSUADE	5. Persuade against (an action)
UNADULTERATED	6. Pure
STILLBORN	7. Dead when delivered from the womb
ORNERY	8. Mischievous
PROMETHEUS	9. Titan in Greek mythology who steals fire from heaven for the benefit of mankind
BERSERK	10. In a state of violent or destructive rage or frenzy
SPIRE	11. Top of a pointed, tapering object or structure, as a mountain peak
MIGRAINE	12. Intense, periodically returning headache
HANKERING	13. Craving; yearning
AMBUSH	14. Surprise attack from hidden assailants
DESPAIRING	15. Giving up hope
TREACHEROUS	16. Dangerously unstable
OPTIMISTIC	17. Having the tendency to expect the best outcome
CONSOLE	18. Comfort
CAVORTED	19. Pranced
SKEPTICAL	20. Not easily convinced or persuaded; doubtful

Walk Two Moons Vocabulary Fill in the Blanks 3

1. One taken or held prisoner
2. Horrible; frightful
3. Pretend to be ill to escape work
4. In Greek mythology, the first mortal woman; out o curiosity she opens a box
5. Breakfast cereal like granola
6. Demise, destruction or decay
7. Dead when delivered from the womb
8. Not easily convinced or persuaded; doubtful
9. Dangerously unstable
10. Surprise attack from hidden assailants
11. Given or written by a person whose name is unknown
12. Searching thoroughly by moving the contents about
13. Lot; group
14. Bold resistance to authority
15. White sterol found in animal fats. Excessive amounts can cause blocked arteries.
16. Persons addicted to some activity or habit
17. An impelling force, usually from within
18. To a great degree
19. Showing high moral qualities
20. Craving; yearning

Walk Two Moons Vocabulary Fill in the Blanks 3 Answer Key

CAPTIVE	1. One taken or held prisoner
GHASTLY	2. Horrible; frightful
MALINGER	3. Pretend to be ill to escape work
PANDORA	4. In Greek mythology, the first mortal woman; out o curiosity she opens a box
MUESLI	5. Breakfast cereal like granola
RUINATION	6. Demise, destruction or decay
STILLBORN	7. Dead when delivered from the womb
SKEPTICAL	8. Not easily convinced or persuaded; doubtful
TREACHEROUS	9. Dangerously unstable
AMBUSH	10. Surprise attack from hidden assailants
ANONYMOUS	11. Given or written by a person whose name is unknown
RUMMAGING	12. Searching thoroughly by moving the contents about
CABOODLE	13. Lot; group
DEFIANCE	14. Bold resistance to authority
CHOLESTEROL	15. White sterol found in animal fats. Excessive amounts can cause blocked arteries.
FIENDS	16. Persons addicted to some activity or habit
IMPULSE	17. An impelling force, usually from within
EXTENSIVELY	18. To a great degree
NOBLE	19. Showing high moral qualities
HANKERING	20. Craving; yearning

Walk Two Moons Vocabulary Fill in the Blanks 4

_____ 1. Having unlimited power

_____ 2. Adapting a young child or animal to go without something

_____ 3. Bubbling up

_____ 4. Top of a pointed, tapering object or structure, as a mountain peak

_____ 5. Dead when delivered from the womb

_____ 6. Pure

_____ 7. Exciting interest of curiosity

_____ 8. Epidemic diseases that are deadly

_____ 9. To a great degree

_____ 10. U-shaped

_____ 11. Physically weak; delicate

_____ 12. Harassing

_____ 13. Comfort

_____ 14. Legal; proper; within the law

_____ 15. Put into a trance-like condition

_____ 16. Hesitantly

_____ 17. In a state of violent or destructive rage or frenzy

_____ 18. Plentiful

_____ 19. Mischievous

_____ 20. Dangerously unstable

Walk Two Moons Vocabulary Fill in the Blanks 4 Answer Key

OMNIPOTENT	1. Having unlimited power
WEANING	2. Adapting a young child or animal to go without something
PERCOLATING	3. Bubbling up
SPIRE	4. Top of a pointed, tapering object or structure, as a mountain peak
STILLBORN	5. Dead when delivered from the womb
UNADULTERATED	6. Pure
INTRIGUING	7. Exciting interest of curiosity
PLAGUES	8. Epidemic diseases that are deadly
EXTENSIVELY	9. To a great degree
HAIRPIN	10. U-shaped
FRAGILE	11. Physically weak; delicate
BESIEGING	12. Harassing
CONSOLE	13. Comfort
LEGITIMATE	14. Legal; proper; within the law
HYPNOTIZED	15. Put into a trance-like condition
TENTATIVELY	16. Hesitantly
BERSERK	17. In a state of violent or destructive rage or frenzy
BOUNTIFUL	18. Plentiful
ORNERY	19. Mischievous
TREACHEROUS	20. Dangerously unstable

Walk Two Moons Vocabulary Matching 1

___ 1. SPIRE
___ 2. CABOODLE
___ 3. STILLBORN
___ 4. HOLSTER
___ 5. RASPY
___ 6. SPARE
___ 7. MISCELLANEOUS
___ 8. RHODODENDRON
___ 9. DESPAIRING
___ 10. CHOLESTEROL
___ 11. MOURNFULLY
___ 12. DEFIANCE
___ 13. PANDEMONIUM
___ 14. EXTENSIVELY
___ 15. CADAVER
___ 16. FIENDS
___ 17. DEFYING
___ 18. ANONYMOUS
___ 19. BERSERK
___ 20. UNADULTERATED
___ 21. WEANING
___ 22. PROMETHEUS
___ 23. DEPRIVED
___ 24. MOCCASINS
___ 25. CONSOLE

A. Adapting a young child or animal to go without something
B. Soft, heelless, leather slippers originally worn by North American Indians
C. White sterol found in animal fats. Excessive amounts can cause blocked arteries.
D. In a state of violent or destructive rage or frenzy
E. Persons addicted to some activity or habit
F. Dead when delivered from the womb
G. Pure
H. Lot; group
I. Pistol holder
J. Varied; mixed
K. Top of a pointed, tapering object or structure, as a mountain peak
L. Shrub with showy flowers of pink, white, or purple
M. Wild disorder, noise, or confusion
N. Challenging; daring
O. Bold resistance to authority
P. Refrain from troubling or worrying
Q. Grating; easily irritated; rough
R. Comfort
S. To a great degree
T. Dead body
U. Given or written by a person whose name is unknown
V. Giving up hope
W. Sadly
X. Titan in Greek mythology who steals fire from heaven for the benefit of mankind
Y. To have undergone a loss; to not have something

Walk Two Moons Vocabulary Matching 1 Answer Key

K - 1. SPIRE	A.	Adapting a young child or animal to go without something
H - 2. CABOODLE	B.	Soft, heelless, leather slippers originally worn by North American Indians
F - 3. STILLBORN	C.	White sterol found in animal fats. Excessive amounts can cause blocked arteries.
I - 4. HOLSTER	D.	In a state of violent or destructive rage or frenzy
Q - 5. RASPY	E.	Persons addicted to some activity or habit
P - 6. SPARE	F.	Dead when delivered from the womb
J - 7. MISCELLANEOUS	G.	Pure
L - 8. RHODODENDRON	H.	Lot; group
V - 9. DESPAIRING	I.	Pistol holder
C - 10. CHOLESTEROL	J.	Varied; mixed
W - 11. MOURNFULLY	K.	Top of a pointed, tapering object or structure, as a mountain peak
O - 12. DEFIANCE	L.	Shrub with showy flowers of pink, white, or purple
M - 13. PANDEMONIUM	M.	Wild disorder, noise, or confusion
S - 14. EXTENSIVELY	N.	Challenging; daring
T - 15. CADAVER	O.	Bold resistance to authority
E - 16. FIENDS	P.	Refrain from troubling or worrying
N - 17. DEFYING	Q.	Grating; easily irritated; rough
U - 18. ANONYMOUS	R.	Comfort
D - 19. BERSERK	S.	To a great degree
G - 20. UNADULTERATED	T.	Dead body
A - 21. WEANING	U.	Given or written by a person whose name is unknown
X - 22. PROMETHEUS	V.	Giving up hope
Y - 23. DEPRIVED	W.	Sadly
B - 24. MOCCASINS	X.	Titan in Greek mythology who steals fire from heaven for the benefit of mankind
R - 25. CONSOLE	Y.	To have undergone a loss; to not have something

Walk Two Moons Vocabulary Matching 2

___ 1. FIENDS   A. Shrub with showy flowers of pink, white, or purple
___ 2. MOCCASINS   B. Knotty & twisted, as in the trunk of an old tree
___ 3. DEFYING   C. Mischievous
___ 4. MALINGER   D. In Greek mythology, the first mortal woman; out o curiosity she opens a box
___ 5. BERSERK   E. In a state of violent or destructive rage or frenzy
___ 6. CAVORTED   F. Challenging; daring
___ 7. CAPTIVE   G. Soft, heelless, leather slippers originally worn by North American Indians
___ 8. OPTIMISTIC   H. Grating; easily irritated; rough
___ 9. ORNERY   I. Having the tendency to expect the best outcome
___10. TREACHEROUS   J. Deceived
___11. DEPRIVED   K. Physically weak; delicate
___12. PANDORA   L. Refrain from troubling or worrying
___13. DIABOLIC   M. One taken or held prisoner
___14. OMNIPOTENT   N. Adapting a young child or animal to go without something
___15. BETRAYED   O. Having unlimited power
___16. PIOUS   P. Having or showing religious devotion
___17. RHODODENDRON   Q. Very wicked or cruel
___18. GNARLED   R. Deep narrow passes between steep heights
___19. FRAGILE   S. To have undergone a loss; to not have something
___20. WEANING   T. Pure
___21. UNADULTERATED   U. Comfort
___22. CONSOLE   V. Pretend to be ill to escape work
___23. RASPY   W. Dangerously unstable
___24. SPARE   X. Persons addicted to some activity or habit
___25. GORGES   Y. Pranced

Walk Two Moons Vocabulary Matching 2 Answer Key

X - 1.	FIENDS	A. Shrub with showy flowers of pink, white, or purple
G - 2.	MOCCASINS	B. Knotty & twisted, as in the trunk of an old tree
F - 3.	DEFYING	C. Mischievous
V - 4.	MALINGER	D. In Greek mythology, the first mortal woman; out o curiosity she opens a box
E - 5.	BERSERK	E. In a state of violent or destructive rage or frenzy
Y - 6.	CAVORTED	F. Challenging; daring
M - 7.	CAPTIVE	G. Soft, heelless, leather slippers originally worn by North American Indians
I - 8.	OPTIMISTIC	H. Grating; easily irritated; rough
C - 9.	ORNERY	I. Having the tendency to expect the best outcome
W -10.	TREACHEROUS	J. Deceived
S -11.	DEPRIVED	K. Physically weak; delicate
D -12.	PANDORA	L. Refrain from troubling or worrying
Q -13.	DIABOLIC	M. One taken or held prisoner
O -14.	OMNIPOTENT	N. Adapting a young child or animal to go without something
J -15.	BETRAYED	O. Having unlimited power
P -16.	PIOUS	P. Having or showing religious devotion
A -17.	RHODODENDRON	Q. Very wicked or cruel
B -18.	GNARLED	R. Deep narrow passes between steep heights
K -19.	FRAGILE	S. To have undergone a loss; to not have something
N -20.	WEANING	T. Pure
T -21.	UNADULTERATED	U. Comfort
U -22.	CONSOLE	V. Pretend to be ill to escape work
H -23.	RASPY	W. Dangerously unstable
L -24.	SPARE	X. Persons addicted to some activity or habit
R -25.	GORGES	Y. Pranced

Walk Two Moons Vocabulary Matching 3

___ 1. MALINGER
___ 2. ACCUMULATED
___ 3. RUINATION
___ 4. AMBUSH
___ 5. PROMETHEUS
___ 6. UNADULTERATED
___ 7. STILLBORN
___ 8. COLOSSAL
___ 9. BOUNTIFUL
___ 10. BERSERK
___ 11. DEFENSIVE
___ 12. PIOUS
___ 13. MANNA
___ 14. GHASTLY
___ 15. AMNESIA
___ 16. ORNERY
___ 17. ELABORATE
___ 18. SKEPTICAL
___ 19. SPIRE
___ 20. HYPNOTIZED
___ 21. CABOODLE
___ 22. OPTIMISTIC
___ 23. INTRIGUING
___ 24. SULLEN
___ 25. RHODODENDRON

A. In a state of violent or destructive rage or frenzy
B. Pure
C. Huge; gigantic
D. Horrible; frightful
E. Gloomy; dismal
F. Add more details
G. Pretend to be ill to escape work
H. Divine aids; spiritual sustenance
I. Titan in Greek mythology who steals fire from heaven for the benefit of mankind
J. Exciting interest of curiosity
K. Lot; group
L. Collected or gathered together
M. Mischievous
N. Plentiful
O. Surprise attack from hidden assailants
P. Not easily convinced or persuaded; doubtful
Q. Having the tendency to expect the best outcome
R. Top of a pointed, tapering object or structure, as a mountain peak
S. Having or showing religious devotion
T. Dead when delivered from the womb
U. Demise, destruction or decay
V. Partial or total loss of memory caused by brain injury or shock
W. Feeling under attack and hence quick to justify one's actions
X. Put into a trance-like condition
Y. Shrub with showy flowers of pink, white, or purple

Walk Two Moons Vocabulary Matching 3 Answer Key

G - 1.	MALINGER	A. In a state of violent or destructive rage or frenzy
L - 2.	ACCUMULATED	B. Pure
U - 3.	RUINATION	C. Huge; gigantic
O - 4.	AMBUSH	D. Horrible; frightful
I - 5.	PROMETHEUS	E. Gloomy; dismal
B - 6.	UNADULTERATED	F. Add more details
T - 7.	STILLBORN	G. Pretend to be ill to escape work
C - 8.	COLOSSAL	H. Divine aids; spiritual sustenance
N - 9.	BOUNTIFUL	I. Titan in Greek mythology who steals fire from heaven for the benefit of mankind
A - 10.	BERSERK	J. Exciting interest of curiosity
W - 11.	DEFENSIVE	K. Lot; group
S - 12.	PIOUS	L. Collected or gathered together
H - 13.	MANNA	M. Mischievous
D - 14.	GHASTLY	N. Plentiful
V - 15.	AMNESIA	O. Surprise attack from hidden assailants
M - 16.	ORNERY	P. Not easily convinced or persuaded; doubtful
F - 17.	ELABORATE	Q. Having the tendency to expect the best outcome
P - 18.	SKEPTICAL	R. Top of a pointed, tapering object or structure, as a mountain peak
R - 19.	SPIRE	S. Having or showing religious devotion
X - 20.	HYPNOTIZED	T. Dead when delivered from the womb
K - 21.	CABOODLE	U. Demise, destruction or decay
Q - 22.	OPTIMISTIC	V. Partial or total loss of memory caused by brain injury or shock
J - 23.	INTRIGUING	W. Feeling under attack and hence quick to justify one's actions
E - 24.	SULLEN	X. Put into a trance-like condition
Y - 25.	RHODODENDRON	Y. Shrub with showy flowers of pink, white, or purple

Walk Two Moons Vocabulary Matching 4

___ 1. HORRID
___ 2. ELABORATE
___ 3. MANNA
___ 4. PLAGUES
___ 5. DEPRIVED
___ 6. CADAVER
___ 7. EXTENSIVELY
___ 8. RASPY
___ 9. LEGITIMATE
___ 10. FIENDS
___ 11. SULLEN
___ 12. CABOODLE
___ 13. BOUNTIFUL
___ 14. REASSURANCE
___ 15. HYPNOTIZED
___ 16. PANDORA
___ 17. PANDEMONIUM
___ 18. GHASTLY
___ 19. ACCUMULATED
___ 20. PERCOLATING
___ 21. AMNESIA
___ 22. BADGERED
___ 23. CAVORTED
___ 24. DIABOLIC
___ 25. SPIRE

A. Gloomy; dismal
B. Wild disorder, noise, or confusion
C. Plentiful
D. Grating; easily irritated; rough
E. Add more details
F. Legal; proper; within the law
G. Dead body
H. Pranced
I. Epidemic diseases that are deadly
J. Pestered
K. Divine aids; spiritual sustenance
L. Persons addicted to some activity or habit
M. Bubbling up
N. Causing a feeling of horror; ugly; unpleasant
O. In Greek mythology, the first mortal woman; out o curiosity she opens a box
P. To have undergone a loss; to not have something
Q. Put into a trance-like condition
R. Top of a pointed, tapering object or structure, as a mountain peak
S. Restored confidence
T. Partial or total loss of memory caused by brain injury or shock
U. Lot; group
V. Horrible; frightful
W. Collected or gathered together
X. Very wicked or cruel
Y. To a great degree

Walk Two Moons Vocabulary Matching 4 Answer Key

N - 1. HORRID	A.	Gloomy; dismal
E - 2. ELABORATE	B.	Wild disorder, noise, or confusion
K - 3. MANNA	C.	Plentiful
I - 4. PLAGUES	D.	Grating; easily irritated; rough
P - 5. DEPRIVED	E.	Add more details
G - 6. CADAVER	F.	Legal; proper; within the law
Y - 7. EXTENSIVELY	G.	Dead body
D - 8. RASPY	H.	Pranced
F - 9. LEGITIMATE	I.	Epidemic diseases that are deadly
L - 10. FIENDS	J.	Pestered
A - 11. SULLEN	K.	Divine aids; spiritual sustenance
U - 12. CABOODLE	L.	Persons addicted to some activity or habit
C - 13. BOUNTIFUL	M.	Bubbling up
S - 14. REASSURANCE	N.	Causing a feeling of horror; ugly; unpleasant
Q - 15. HYPNOTIZED	O.	In Greek mythology, the first mortal woman; out o curiosity she opens a box
O - 16. PANDORA	P.	To have undergone a loss; to not have something
B - 17. PANDEMONIUM	Q.	Put into a trance-like condition
V - 18. GHASTLY	R.	Top of a pointed, tapering object or structure, as a mountain peak
W - 19. ACCUMULATED	S.	Restored confidence
M - 20. PERCOLATING	T.	Partial or total loss of memory caused by brain injury or shock
T - 21. AMNESIA	U.	Lot; group
J - 22. BADGERED	V.	Horrible; frightful
H - 23. CAVORTED	W.	Collected or gathered together
X - 24. DIABOLIC	X.	Very wicked or cruel
R - 25. SPIRE	Y.	To a great degree

Walk Two Moons Vocabulary Magic Squares 1

Match the definition with the vocabulary word. Put your answers in the magic squares below. When your answers are correct, all columns and rows will add to the same number.

A. GNARLED
B. HYPNOTIZED
C. ACCUMULATED
D. SPARE
E. BERSERK
F. DEFIANCE
G. CRUCIAL
H. NOBLE
I. EMBEDDED
J. FRAGILE
K. STILLBORN
L. TREACHEROUS
M. AMNESIA
N. DEPRIVED
O. IMPULSE
P. GORGES

1. An impelling force, usually from within
2. Refrain from troubling or worrying
3. Physically weak; delicate
4. In a state of violent or destructive rage or frenzy
5. Set or fixed firmly
6. Bold resistance to authority
7. Deep narrow passes between steep heights
8. Collected or gathered together
9. Showing high moral qualities
10. Dead when delivered from the womb
11. Knotty & twisted, as in the trunk of an old tree
12. To have undergone a loss; to not have something
13. Put into a trance-like condition
14. Partial or total loss of memory caused by brain injury or shock
15. Of supreme importance
16. Dangerously unstable

A=	B=	C=	D=
E=	F=	G=	H=
I=	J=	K=	L=
M=	N=	O=	P=

Walk Two Moons Vocabulary Magic Squares 1 Answer Key

Match the definition with the vocabulary word. Put your answers in the magic squares below. When your answers are correct, all columns and rows will add to the same number.

A. GNARLED
B. HYPNOTIZED
C. ACCUMULATED
D. SPARE
E. BERSERK
F. DEFIANCE
G. CRUCIAL
H. NOBLE
I. EMBEDDED
J. FRAGILE
K. STILLBORN
L. TREACHEROUS
M. AMNESIA
N. DEPRIVED
O. IMPULSE
P. GORGES

1. An impelling force, usually from within
2. Refrain from troubling or worrying
3. Physically weak; delicate
4. In a state of violent or destructive rage or frenzy
5. Set or fixed firmly
6. Bold resistance to authority
7. Deep narrow passes between steep heights
8. Collected or gathered together
9. Showing high moral qualities
10. Dead when delivered from the womb
11. Knotty & twisted, as in the trunk of an old tree
12. To have undergone a loss; to not have something
13. Put into a trance-like condition
14. Partial or total loss of memory caused by brain injury or shock
15. Of supreme importance
16. Dangerously unstable

A=11	B=13	C=8	D=2
E=4	F=6	G=15	H=9
I=5	J=3	K=10	L=16
M=14	N=12	O=1	P=7

Walk Two Moons Vocabulary Magic Squares 2

Match the definition with the vocabulary word. Put your answers in the magic squares below. When your answers are correct, all columns and rows will add to the same number.

A. FRAGILE
B. OMNIPOTENT
C. DIABOLIC
D. NOBLE
E. LEGITIMATE
F. DEPRIVED
G. PANDORA
H. UNADULTERATED
I. MISCELLANEOUS
J. SKEPTICAL
K. CADAVER
L. HYPNOTIZED
M. ELABORATE
N. BETRAYED
O. MIGRAINE
P. RHODODENDRON

1. Physically weak; delicate
2. Deceived
3. Not easily convinced or persuaded; doubtful
4. Legal; proper; within the law
5. In Greek mythology, the first mortal woman; out o curiosity she opens a box
6. Put into a trance-like condition
7. Shrub with showy flowers of pink, white, or purple
8. Very wicked or cruel
9. Intense, periodically returning headache
10. Showing high moral qualities
11. Pure
12. Dead body
13. Varied; mixed
14. To have undergone a loss; to not have something
15. Having unlimited power
16. Add more details

A=	B=	C=	D=
E=	F=	G=	H=
I=	J=	K=	L=
M=	N=	O=	P=

Walk Two Moons Vocabulary Magic Squares 2 Answer Key

Match the definition with the vocabulary word. Put your answers in the magic squares below. When your answers are correct, all columns and rows will add to the same number.

A. FRAGILE
B. OMNIPOTENT
C. DIABOLIC
D. NOBLE
E. LEGITIMATE
F. DEPRIVED
G. PANDORA
H. UNADULTERATED
I. MISCELLANEOUS
J. SKEPTICAL
K. CADAVER
L. HYPNOTIZED
M. ELABORATE
N. BETRAYED
O. MIGRAINE
P. RHODODENDRON

1. Physically weak; delicate
2. Deceived
3. Not easily convinced or persuaded; doubtful
4. Legal; proper; within the law
5. In Greek mythology, the first mortal woman; out o curiosity she opens a box
6. Put into a trance-like condition
7. Shrub with showy flowers of pink, white, or purple
8. Very wicked or cruel
9. Intense, periodically returning headache
10. Showing high moral qualities
11. Pure
12. Dead body
13. Varied; mixed
14. To have undergone a loss; to not have something
15. Having unlimited power
16. Add more details

A=1	B=15	C=8	D=10
E=4	F=14	G=5	H=11
I=13	J=3	K=12	L=6
M=16	N=2	O=9	P=7

Walk Two Moons Vocabulary Magic Squares 3

Match the definition with the vocabulary word. Put your answers in the magic squares below. When your answers are correct, all columns and rows will add to the same number.

A. IMPULSE
B. PANDEMONIUM
C. PANDORA
D. MALEVOLENT
E. DEFYING
F. SPIRE
G. EMBEDDED
H. RHODODENDRON
I. FRAGILE
J. CRUCIAL
K. ACCUMULATED
L. DEFENSIVE
M. MALINGER
N. AMBUSH
O. BADGERED
P. MUESLI

1. Surprise attack from hidden assailants
2. Set or fixed firmly
3. Feeling under attack and hence quick to justify one's actions
4. An impelling force, usually from within
5. Collected or gathered together
6. Wild disorder, noise, or confusion
7. Pretend to be ill to escape work
8. Shrub with showy flowers of pink, white, or purple
9. Challenging; daring
10. Breakfast cereal like granola
11. In Greek mythology, the first mortal woman; out o curiosity she opens a box
12. Of supreme importance
13. Wishing evil or harm to others
14. Physically weak; delicate
15. Top of a pointed, tapering object or structure, as a mountain peak
16. Pestered

A=	B=	C=	D=
E=	F=	G=	H=
I=	J=	K=	L=
M=	N=	O=	P=

Walk Two Moons Vocabulary Magic Squares 3 Answer Key

Match the definition with the vocabulary word. Put your answers in the magic squares below. When your answers are correct, all columns and rows will add to the same number.

A. IMPULSE
B. PANDEMONIUM
C. PANDORA
D. MALEVOLENT
E. DEFYING
F. SPIRE
G. EMBEDDED
H. RHODODENDRON
I. FRAGILE
J. CRUCIAL
K. ACCUMULATED
L. DEFENSIVE
M. MALINGER
N. AMBUSH
O. BADGERED
P. MUESLI

1. Surprise attack from hidden assailants
2. Set or fixed firmly
3. Feeling under attack and hence quick to justify one's actions
4. An impelling force, usually from within
5. Collected or gathered together
6. Wild disorder, noise, or confusion
7. Pretend to be ill to escape work
8. Shrub with showy flowers of pink, white, or purple
9. Challenging; daring
10. Breakfast cereal like granola
11. In Greek mythology, the first mortal woman; out o curiosity she opens a box
12. Of supreme importance
13. Wishing evil or harm to others
14. Physically weak; delicate
15. Top of a pointed, tapering object or structure, as a mountain peak
16. Pestered

A=4	B=6	C=11	D=13
E=9	F=15	G=2	H=8
I=14	J=12	K=5	L=3
M=7	N=1	O=16	P=10

Walk Two Moons Vocabulary Magic Squares 4

Match the definition with the vocabulary word. Put your answers in the magic squares below. When your answers are correct, all columns and rows will add to the same number.

A. DISSUADE
B. PERCOLATING
C. UNADULTERATED
D. RUINATION
E. EXTENSIVELY
F. CHOLESTEROL
G. CADAVER
H. CONSOLE
I. HOLSTER
J. ACCUMULATED
K. OPTIMISTIC
L. RASPY
M. OMNIPOTENT
N. WEANING
O. MOURNFULLY
P. HANKERING

1. Bubbling up
2. Dead body
3. Having the tendency to expect the best outcome
4. Adapting a young child or animal to go without something
5. Having unlimited power
6. Grating; easily irritated; rough
7. Comfort
8. Persuade against (an action)
9. Craving; yearning
10. Pistol holder
11. To a great degree
12. Demise, destruction or decay
13. Pure
14. White sterol found in animal fats. Excessive amounts can cause blocked arteries.
15. Collected or gathered together
16. Sadly

A= 8	B= 1	C= 13	D= 12
E= 11	F= 14	G= 2	H= 7
I= 10	J= 15	K= 3	L= 6
M= 5	N= 4	O= 16	P= 9

Walk Two Moons Vocabulary Magic Squares 4 Answer Key

Match the definition with the vocabulary word. Put your answers in the magic squares below. When your answers are correct, all columns and rows will add to the same number.

A. DISSUADE
B. PERCOLATING
C. UNADULTERATED
D. RUINATION
E. EXTENSIVELY
F. CHOLESTEROL
G. CADAVER
H. CONSOLE
I. HOLSTER
J. ACCUMULATED
K. OPTIMISTIC
L. RASPY
M. OMNIPOTENT
N. WEANING
O. MOURNFULLY
P. HANKERING

1. Bubbling up
2. Dead body
3. Having the tendency to expect the best outcome
4. Adapting a young child or animal to go without something
5. Having unlimited power
6. Grating; easily irritated; rough
7. Comfort
8. Persuade against (an action)
9. Craving; yearning
10. Pistol holder
11. To a great degree
12. Demise, destruction or decay
13. Pure
14. White sterol found in animal fats. Excessive amounts can cause blocked arteries.
15. Collected or gathered together
16. Sadly

A=8	B=1	C=13	D=12
E=11	F=14	G=2	H=7
I=10	J=15	K=3	L=6
M=5	N=4	O=16	P=9

Walk Two Moons Vocabulary Word Search 1

```
M D O G X F M O C C A S I N S P H F Q J
A E P B M R A W R A C R P W G R Y Q A Q
N F T F S A L E L P A D V B H O P C M L
N Y I G S G E A L T B B V R A M N I B H
A I M O S I V N F I O K R P S E O M U X
C N I R P L O I X V O V B I T T T P S J
R G S G A E L N S E D D X O L H I U H N
Q U T E R G E G D K L B I U Y E Z L O J
C H I S E L N O B L E R E S M U E S L I
A A C N U L T A R O C P A S S S D E S R
V M D G A L A L R N U R T S I U Z Y T H
O N C A H T L B E L E N U I P E A T E B
R E C X V S I E O G E R T C C Y G D R J
T S O Y C E H O N R I D Y I I A T I E G
E I N B K Q R O N V A T F J F A L A N Q
D A S B E R S E R K D T I J Z U L B J G
R H O D O D E N D R O N E M Y H L O Y G
M A L I N G E R N V I H N H A G B L S B
J D E F I A N C E G X D D K L T J I M H
A C C U M U L A T E D D S P I R E C L R
```

Adapting a young child or animal to go without something (7)
Add more details (9)
An impelling force, usually from within (7)
Bold resistance to authority (8)
Breakfast cereal like granola (6)
Causing a feeling of horror; ugly; unpleasant (6)
Challenging; daring (7)
Collected or gathered together (11)
Comfort (7)
Dead body (7)
Deep narrow passes between steep heights (6)
Demise, destruction or decay (9)
Divine aids; spiritual sustenance (5)
Gloomy; dismal (6)
Grating; easily irritated; rough (5)
Hand tool with a sharp, wedged blade (6)
Harassing (9)
Having or showing religious devotion (5)
Having the tendency to expect the best outcome (10)
Horrible; frightful (7)
In a state of violent or destructive rage or frenzy (7)
Knotty & twisted, as in the trunk of an old tree (7)
Legal; proper; within the law (10)
Lot; group (8)
Mischievous (6)
Not easily convinced or persuaded; doubtful (9)
Of supreme importance (7)
One taken or held prisoner (7)
Partial or total loss of memory caused by brain injury or shock (7)
Persons addicted to some activity or habit (6)
Persuade against (an action) (8)
Physically weak; delicate (7)
Pistol holder (7)
Plentiful (9)
Pranced (8)
Pretend to be ill to escape work (8)
Put into a trance-like condition (10)
Refrain from troubling or worrying (5)
Showing high moral qualities (5)
Shrub with showy flowers of pink, white, or purple (12)
Soft, heelless, leather slippers originally worn by North American Indians (9)
Surprise attack from hidden assailants (6)
Titan in Greek mythology who steals fire from heaven for the benefit of mankind (10)
Top of a pointed, tapering object or structure, as a mountain peak (5)
Very wicked or cruel (8)
Wishing evil or harm to others (10)

Walk Two Moons Vocabulary Word Search 1 Answer Key

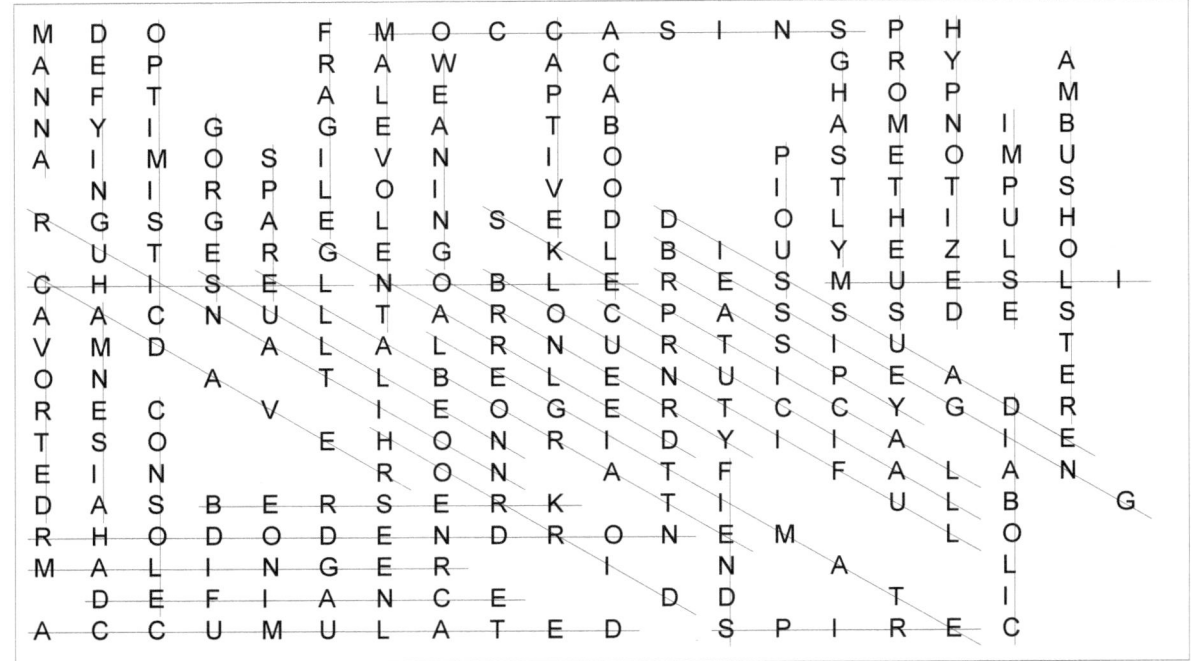

Adapting a young child or animal to go without something (7)
Add more details (9)
An impelling force, usually from within (7)
Bold resistance to authority (8)
Breakfast cereal like granola (6)
Causing a feeling of horror; ugly; unpleasant (6)
Challenging; daring (7)
Collected or gathered together (11)
Comfort (7)
Dead body (7)
Deep narrow passes between steep heights (6)
Demise, destruction or decay (9)
Divine aids; spiritual sustenance (5)
Gloomy; dismal (6)
Grating; easily irritated; rough (5)
Hand tool with a sharp, wedged blade (6)
Harassing (9)
Having or showing religious devotion (5)
Having the tendency to expect the best outcome (10)
Horrible; frightful (7)
In a state of violent or destructive rage or frenzy (7)
Knotty & twisted, as in the trunk of an old tree (7)
Legal; proper; within the law (10)
Lot; group (8)
Mischievous (6)

Not easily convinced or persuaded; doubtful (9)
Of supreme importance (7)
One taken or held prisoner (7)
Partial or total loss of memory caused by brain injury or shock (7)
Persons addicted to some activity or habit (6)
Persuade against (an action) (8)
Physically weak; delicate (7)
Pistol holder (7)
Plentiful (9)
Pranced (8)
Pretend to be ill to escape work (8)
Put into a trance-like condition (10)
Refrain from troubling or worrying (5)
Showing high moral qualities (5)
Shrub with showy flowers of pink, white, or purple (12)
Soft, heelless, leather slippers originally worn by North American Indians (9)
Surprise attack from hidden assailants (6)
Titan in Greek mythology who steals fire from heaven for the benefit of mankind (10)
Top of a pointed, tapering object or structure, as a mountain peak (5)
Very wicked or cruel (8)
Wishing evil or harm to others (10)

Walk Two Moons Vocabulary Word Search 2

```
S C O L O S S A L C M A N O N Y M O U S
Q U F H R D K Y B A A P D M G O R G E S
M N L R Z N E C G D N A E N H O R R I D
J R S L A W P W N A N F I E N D S M Y
C A P P E G T Y A V A D I P M X N N O F
Q S I L O N I V R E S O A O B P M Z U M
C P R A R D C L L R D R N T E R I R R Y
B Y E G N E A F E P H A C E D O G H N R
K E F U E S L P D P I O E N D M R A F J
M C R E R P M M S C F O L T E E A N U T
R R R S Y A S U G O Y V U S D T I K L W
D U V R E I D H E N T B C S T H N E L Q
I C M F G R E A S S U R A N C E E R Y F
S I H M H I K I N O L N P M T U R I M Z
S A Y I A N M R F L F I T Y B S Q N B D
U L N T S G G P W E A N I N G U P G G N
A Z N W T E I I U C P O V N S L S A R W
D C L D L G L N S L Y B E G T L C H R R
E D E F Y I N G G M S L A M N E S I A E
T E N T A T I V E L Y E D I A B O L I C
```

Adapting a young child or animal to go without something (7)
An impelling force, usually from within (7)
Bold resistance to authority (8)
Breakfast cereal like granola (6)
Causing a feeling of horror; ugly; unpleasant (6)
Challenging; daring (7)
Comfort (7)
Craving; yearning (9)
Dead body (7)
Deep narrow passes between steep heights (6)
Divine aids; spiritual sustenance (5)
Epidemic diseases that are deadly (7)
Given or written by a person whose name is unknown (9)
Giving up hope (10)
Gloomy; dismal (6)
Grating; easily irritated; rough (5)
Hand tool with a sharp, wedged blade (6)
Having or showing religious devotion (5)
Having unlimited power (10)
Hesitantly (11)
Horrible; frightful (7)
Huge; gigantic (8)
In Greek mythology, the first mortal woman; out o curiosity she opens a box (7)
In a state of violent or destructive rage or frenzy (7)
Intense, periodically returning headache (8)
Knotty & twisted, as in the trunk of an old tree (7)
Mischievous (6)
Not easily convinced or persuaded; doubtful (9)
Of supreme importance (7)
One taken or held prisoner (7)
Partial or total loss of memory caused by brain injury or shock (7)
Persons addicted to some activity or habit (6)
Persuade against (an action) (8)
Physically weak; delicate (7)
Pistol holder (7)
Refrain from troubling or worrying (5)
Restored confidence (11)
Sadly (10)
Searching thoroughly by moving the contents about (9)
Set or fixed firmly (8)
Showing high moral qualities (5)
Surprise attack from hidden assailants (6)
Titan in Greek mythology who steals fire from heaven for the benefit of mankind (10)
Top of a pointed, tapering object or structure, as a mountain peak (5)
U-shaped (7)
Very wicked or cruel (8)

Walk Two Moons Vocabulary Word Search 2 Answer Key

Adapting a young child or animal to go without something (7)
An impelling force, usually from within (7)
Bold resistance to authority (8)
Breakfast cereal like granola (6)
Causing a feeling of horror; ugly; unpleasant (6)
Challenging; daring (7)
Comfort (7)
Craving; yearning (9)
Dead body (7)
Deep narrow passes between steep heights (6)
Divine aids; spiritual sustenance (5)
Epidemic diseases that are deadly (7)
Given or written by a person whose name is unknown (9)
Giving up hope (10)
Gloomy; dismal (6)
Grating; easily irritated; rough (5)
Hand tool with a sharp, wedged blade (6)
Having or showing religious devotion (5)
Having unlimited power (10)
Hesitantly (11)
Horrible; frightful (7)
Huge; gigantic (8)
In Greek mythology, the first mortal woman; out o curiosity she opens a box (7)
In a state of violent or destructive rage or frenzy (7)

Intense, periodically returning headache (8)
Knotty & twisted, as in the trunk of an old tree (7)
Mischievous (6)
Not easily convinced or persuaded; doubtful (9)
Of supreme importance (7)
One taken or held prisoner (7)
Partial or total loss of memory caused by brain injury or shock (7)
Persons addicted to some activity or habit (6)
Persuade against (an action) (8)
Physically weak; delicate (7)
Pistol holder (7)
Refrain from troubling or worrying (5)
Restored confidence (11)
Sadly (10)
Searching thoroughly by moving the contents about (9)
Set or fixed firmly (8)
Showing high moral qualities (5)
Surprise attack from hidden assailants (6)
Titan in Greek mythology who steals fire from heaven for the benefit of mankind (10)
Top of a pointed, tapering object or structure, as a mountain peak (5)
U-shaped (7)
Very wicked or cruel (8)

Walk Two Moons Vocabulary Word Search 3

```
H  A  N  K  E  R  I  N  G  S  M  A  N  O  N  Y  M  O  U  S
C  C  Q  W  E  A  N  I  N  G  I  C  R  U  C  I  A  L  A  Y
O  A  P  K  C  M  G  R  X  T  G  L  R  M  S  E  L  D  M  Q
N  P  D  L  C  W  B  M  O  U  R  N  F  U  L  L  Y  P  N  K
S  T  D  E  A  R  M  M  E  Q  P  A  N  D  O  R  A  B  V  E
O  I  C  E  F  G  H  A  D  M  I  P  Y  B  K  B  O  H  S  V
L  V  Q  A  F  I  U  O  L  D  N  P  X  E  D  O  U  F  I  N
E  E  T  H  D  E  A  E  D  E  E  G  L  T  C  R  N  R  A  W
D  W  X  B  O  A  N  N  S  O  V  D  H  R  H  A  T  A  R  T
L  E  S  G  M  R  V  S  C  Z  D  O  R  A  B  T  I  G  A  D
M  S  F  C  A  S  R  E  I  E  M  E  L  Y  S  E  F  I  S  B
S  T  D  Y  L  N  P  I  R  V  U  N  N  E  F  T  U  L  P  K
Z  I  M  S  I  P  B  A  D  G  E  R  E  D  N  I  L  E  Y  N
J  L  A  T  N  N  X  C  R  Q  S  A  H  E  R  T  E  Y  H  W
T  L  N  Z  G  T  G  P  P  E  L  M  O  P  H  O  R  N  M  V
G  B  N  O  E  I  B  W  R  V  I  B  L  R  A  G  N  S  D  Z
N  O  A  P  R  O  M  E  T  H  E  U  S  I  I  N  S  U  C  S
O  R  R  X  D  N  P  P  R  F  H  S  T  V  R  A  P  L  H  X
B  N  Z  G  J  K  E  I  U  S  H  H  E  E  P  R  I  L  I  D
L  B  Z  K  J  Z  R  O  L  E  Z  R  D  I  L  R  E  S  W
E  F  K  L  V  S  D  Y  Y  U  S  R  T  D  N  E  E  N  E  M
C  O  L  O  S  S  A  L  D  S  S  E  K  H  H  D  D  G  L  D
```

AMBUSH	CRUCIAL	HAIRPIN	ORNERY
AMNESIA	DEFENSIVE	HANKERING	PANDORA
ANONYMOUS	DEFIANCE	HOLSTER	PIOUS
BADGERED	DEFYING	HORRID	PLAGUES
BERSERK	DEPRIVED	IMPULSE	PROMETHEUS
BETRAYED	ELABORATE	MALEVOLENT	RASPY
BOUNTIFUL	EMBEDDED	MALINGER	RHODODENDRON
CADAVER	FIENDS	MANNA	SPARE
CAPTIVE	FRAGILE	MIGRAINE	SPIRE
CHISEL	GHASTLY	MOURNFULLY	STILLBORN
COLOSSAL	GNARLED	MUESLI	SULLEN
CONSOLE	GORGES	NOBLE	WEANING

Copyrighted

Walk Two Moons Vocabulary Word Search 3 Answer Key

AMBUSH	CRUCIAL	HAIRPIN	ORNERY
AMNESIA	DEFENSIVE	HANKERING	PANDORA
ANONYMOUS	DEFIANCE	HOLSTER	PIOUS
BADGERED	DEFYING	HORRID	PLAGUES
BERSERK	DEPRIVED	IMPULSE	PROMETHEUS
BETRAYED	ELABORATE	MALEVOLENT	RASPY
BOUNTIFUL	EMBEDDED	MALINGER	RHODODENDRON
CADAVER	FIENDS	MANNA	SPARE
CAPTIVE	FRAGILE	MIGRAINE	SPIRE
CHISEL	GHASTLY	MOURNFULLY	STILLBORN
COLOSSAL	GNARLED	MUESLI	SULLEN
CONSOLE	GORGES	NOBLE	WEANING

Walk Two Moons Vocabulary Word Search 4

```
A C C U M U L A T E D B P L A G U E S R
C O A R U M Y B A D G E R E D H C B W C
A N B D E F I A N C E S B E T R A Y E D
P S O C S H F G J S K I S G P V V R R G
T O O A L D E P R I V E D P B G O S Y C
I L D D I G R P D A J G G N I G R M G X
V E L A B O R A T E I I P O C R T F P T
E B E V R E L U C T A N T O R N E R Y P
S Z F E X B C S R C D G E G U G D E E C
P M R R Q A O R G A E V T N C M E A M R
A N O N Y M O U S Z S D K A I A C S B F
R M Z L V B J I N G P P S R A L O S E F
E P N R T U Q N G T A H Y L L I L U D B
D H R E Y S J A T C I C V E R N O R D T
E J A O S H D T P P R F H D M G S A E H
F Q J I M I N I Q A I G U I J E S N D W
E B H T R E A O A N N O H L S R A C F G
N O B L E P T N M B G D U A H E L E I F
S J B J B B I H D A O K O S S G L N E M
I M P U L S E N E W N L G R X T V F N W
V S U L L E N Q G U Y N I R A P L M D H
E S T I L L B O R N S Q A C K Q Z Y S J
```

ACCUMULATED   CAPTIVE   DIABOLIC   MANNA   REASSURANCE

AMBUSH   CAVORTED   ELABORATE   MIGRAINE   RELUCTANT

AMNESIA   CHISEL   EMBEDDED   MUESLI   RUINATION

ANONYMOUS   COLOSSAL   FIENDS   NOBLE   SPARE

BADGERED   CONSOLE   GHASTLY   ORNERY   SPIRE

BESIEGING   CRUCIAL   GNARLED   PANDORA   STILLBORN

BETRAYED   DEFENSIVE   GORGES   PIOUS   SULLEN

BOUNTIFUL   DEFIANCE   HAIRPIN   PLAGUES

CABOODLE   DEPRIVED   IMPULSE   PROMETHEUS

CADAVER   DESPAIRING   MALINGER   RASPY

Walk Two Moons Vocabulary Word Search 4 Answer Key

ACCUMULATED	CAPTIVE	DIABOLIC	MANNA	REASSURANCE
AMBUSH	CAVORTED	ELABORATE	MIGRAINE	RELUCTANT
AMNESIA	CHISEL	EMBEDDED	MUESLI	RUINATION
ANONYMOUS	COLOSSAL	FIENDS	NOBLE	SPARE
BADGERED	CONSOLE	GHASTLY	ORNERY	SPIRE
BESIEGING	CRUCIAL	GNARLED	PANDORA	STILLBORN
BETRAYED	DEFENSIVE	GORGES	PIOUS	SULLEN
BOUNTIFUL	DEFIANCE	HAIRPIN	PLAGUES	
CABOODLE	DEPRIVED	IMPULSE	PROMETHEUS	
CADAVER	DESPAIRING	MALINGER	RASPY	

Walk Two Moons Vocabulary Crossword 1

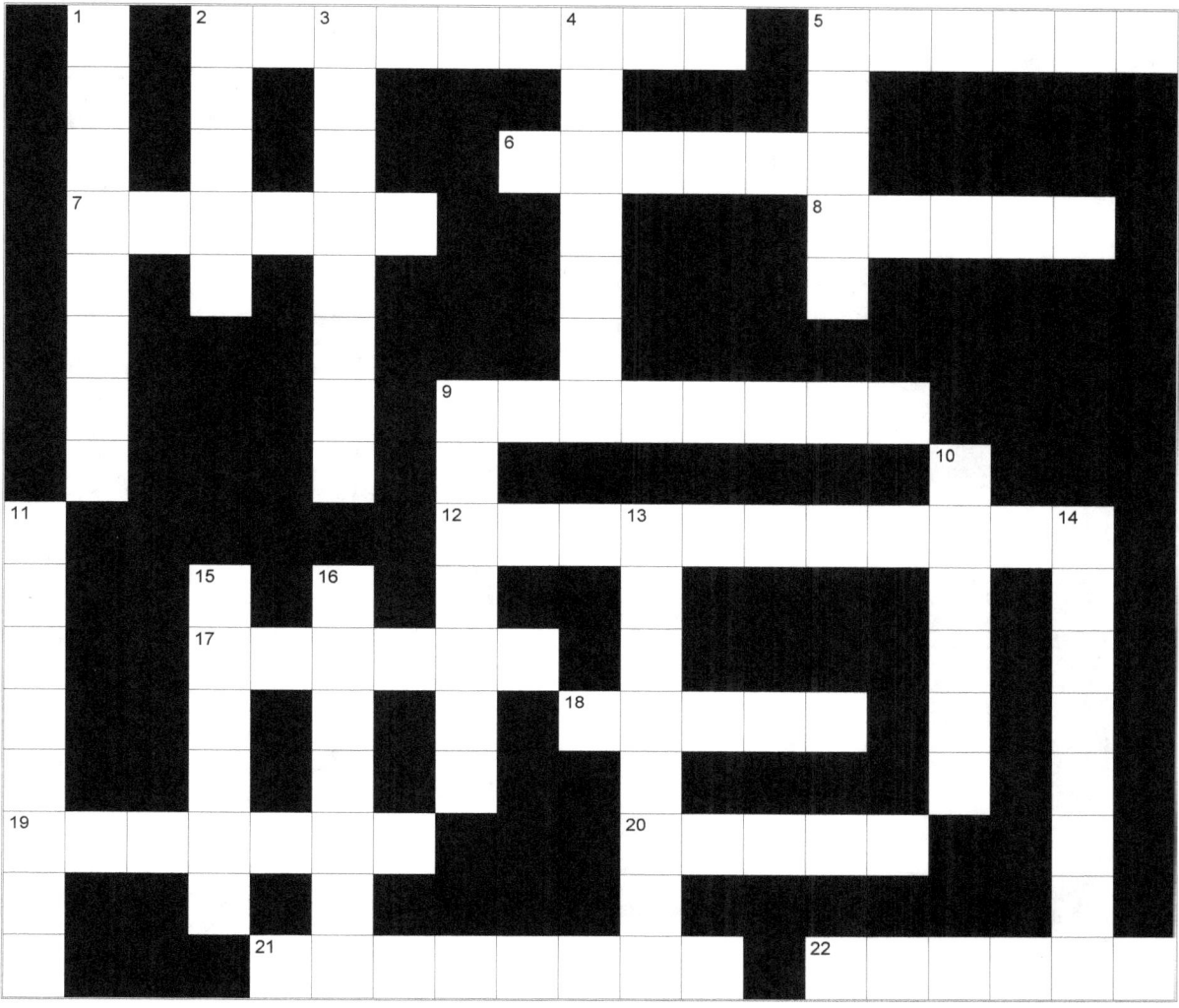

Across
2. Not easily convinced or persuaded; doubtful
5. Gloomy; dismal
6. Breakfast cereal like granola
7. Deep narrow passes between steep heights
8. Grating; easily irritated; rough
9. Huge; gigantic
12. Wild disorder, noise, or confusion
17. Causing a feeling of horror; ugly; unpleasant
18. Having or showing religious devotion
19. Partial or total loss of memory caused by brain injury or shock
20. Showing high moral qualities
21. Deceived
22. Mischievous

Down
1. Pestered
2. Refrain from troubling or worrying
3. Set or fixed firmly
4. Of supreme importance
5. Top of a pointed, tapering object or structure, as a mountain peak
9. One taken or held prisoner
10. Persons addicted to some activity or habit
11. Persuade against (an action)
13. Bold resistance to authority
14. Pretend to be ill to escape work
15. Hand tool with a sharp, wedged blade
16. Physically weak; delicate

Walk Two Moons Vocabulary Crossword 1 Answer Key

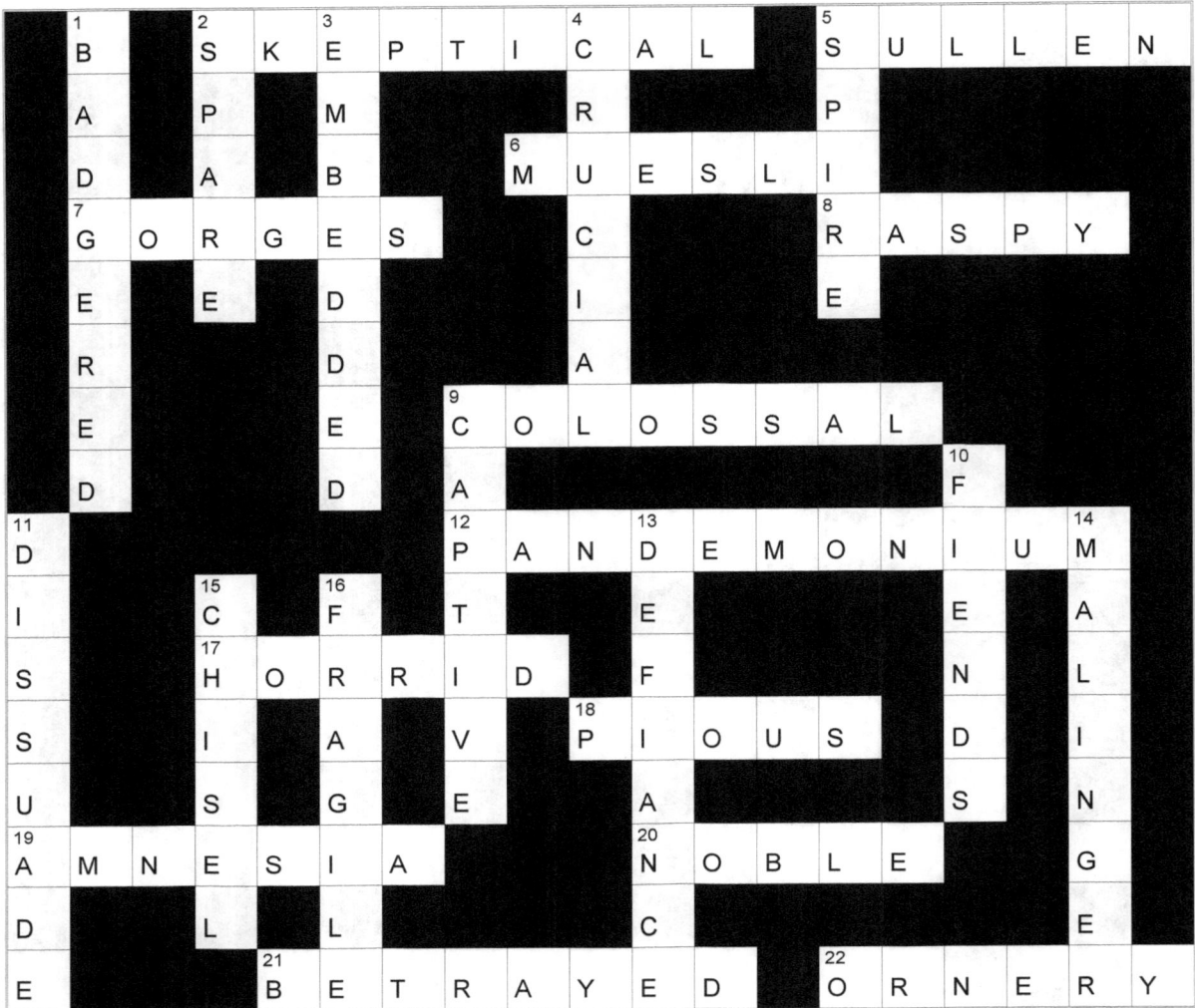

Across
2. Not easily convinced or persuaded; doubtful
5. Gloomy; dismal
6. Breakfast cereal like granola
7. Deep narrow passes between steep heights
8. Grating; easily irritated; rough
9. Huge; gigantic
12. Wild disorder, noise, or confusion
17. Causing a feeling of horror; ugly; unpleasant
18. Having or showing religious devotion
19. Partial or total loss of memory caused by brain injury or shock
20. Showing high moral qualities
21. Deceived
22. Mischievous

Down
1. Pestered
2. Refrain from troubling or worrying
3. Set or fixed firmly
4. Of supreme importance
5. Top of a pointed, tapering object or structure, as a mountain peak
9. One taken or held prisoner
10. Persons addicted to some activity or habit
11. Persuade against (an action)
13. Bold resistance to authority
14. Pretend to be ill to escape work
15. Hand tool with a sharp, wedged blade
16. Physically weak; delicate

Walk Two Moons Vocabulary Crossword 2

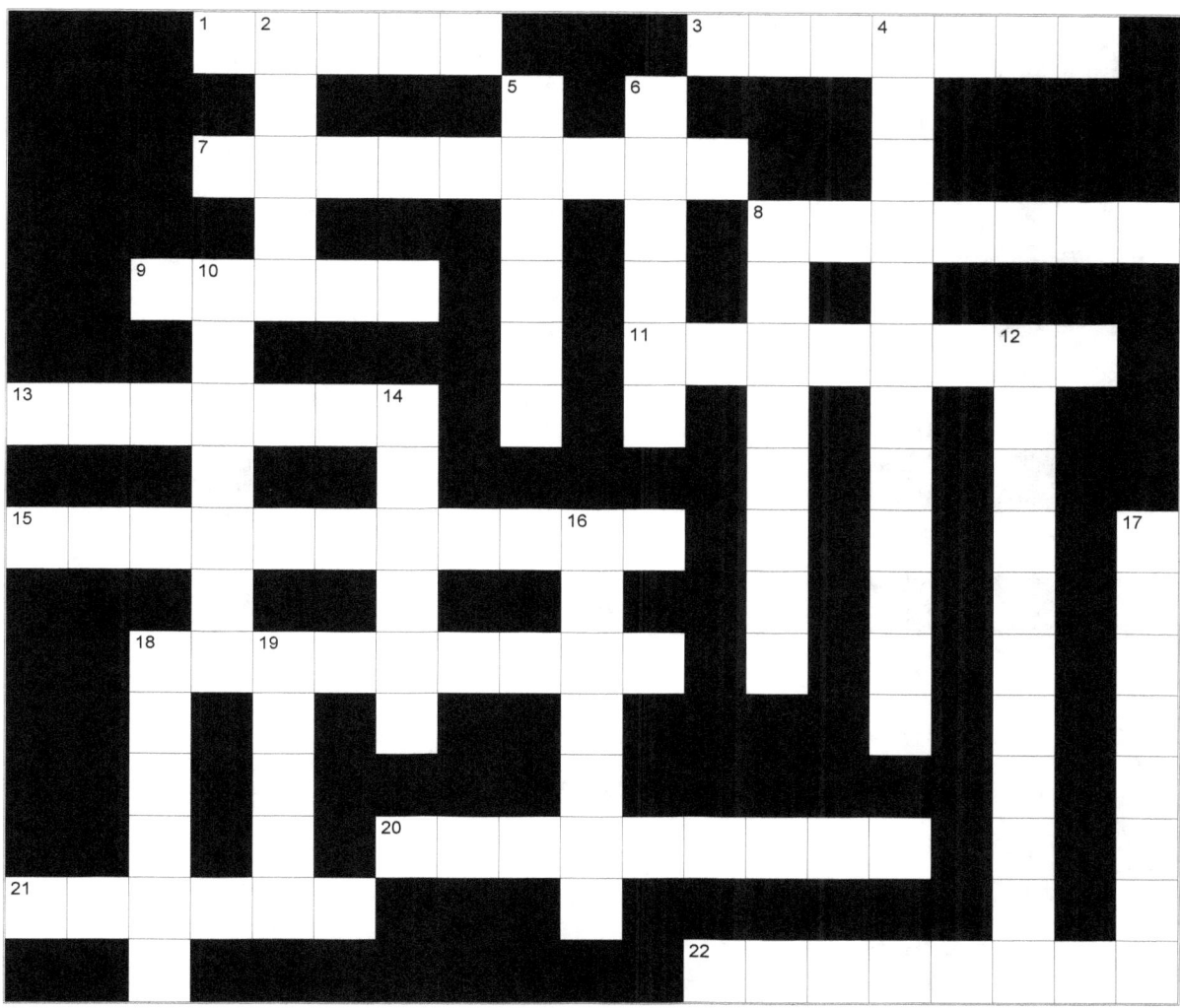

Across
1. Top of a pointed, tapering object or structure, as a mountain peak
3. Knotty & twisted, as in the trunk of an old tree
7. Plentiful
8. Dead body
9. Grating; easily irritated; rough
11. Set or fixed firmly
13. Adapting a young child or animal to go without something
15. Restored confidence
18. Craving; yearning
20. Dead when delivered from the womb
21. Hand tool with a sharp, wedged blade
22. Deceived

Down
2. Having or showing religious devotion
4. Shrub with showy flowers of pink, white, or purple
5. Persons addicted to some activity or habit
6. Gloomy; dismal
8. Lot; group
10. Partial or total loss of memory caused by brain injury or shock
12. To a great degree
14. Deep narrow passes between steep heights
16. Comfort
17. Pestered
18. Causing a feeling of horror; ugly; unpleasant
19. Showing high moral qualities

Walk Two Moons Vocabulary Crossword 2 Answer Key

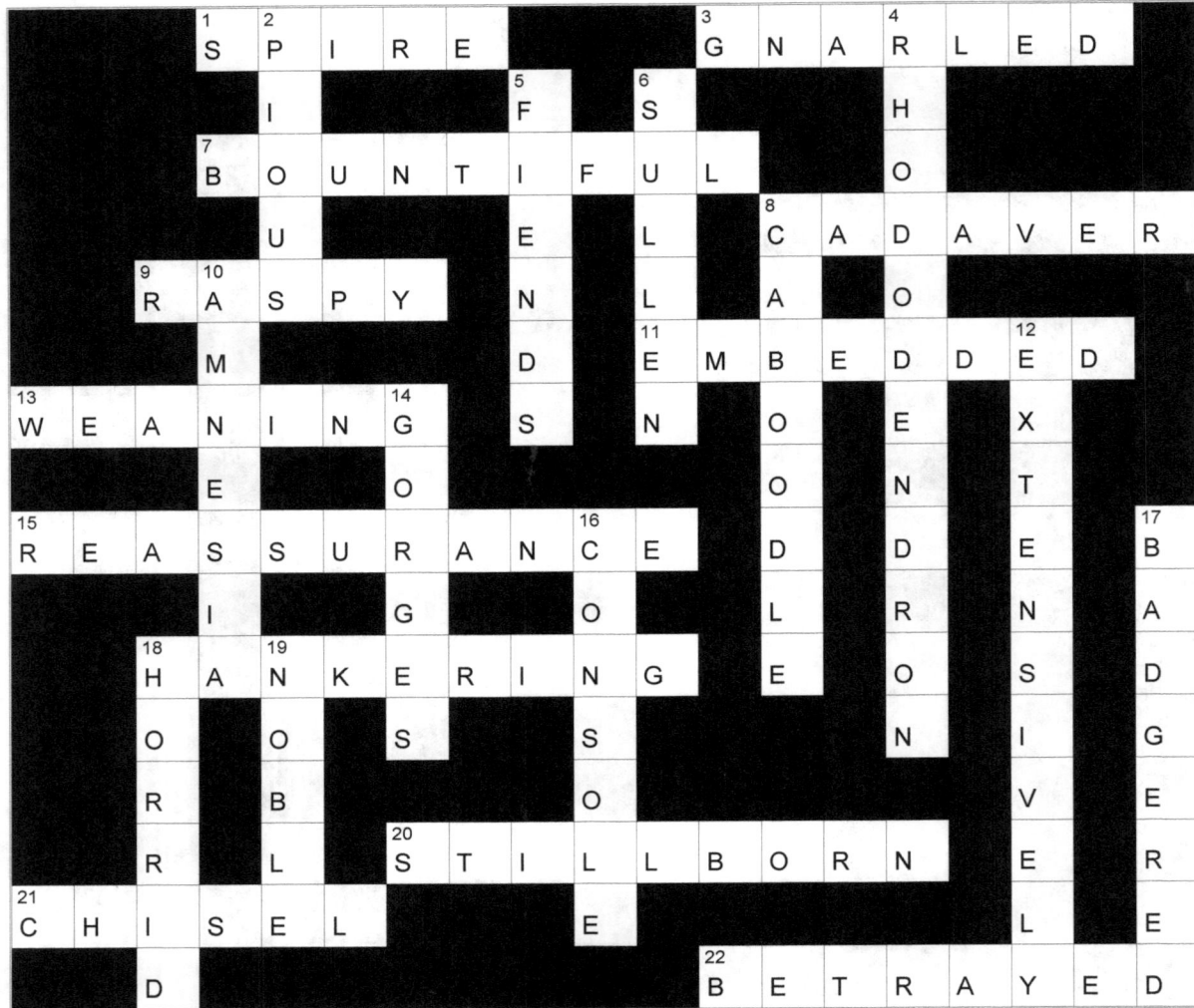

Across
1. Top of a pointed, tapering object or structure, as a mountain peak
3. Knotty & twisted, as in the trunk of an old tree
7. Plentiful
8. Dead body
9. Grating; easily irritated; rough
11. Set or fixed firmly
13. Adapting a young child or animal to go without something
15. Restored confidence
18. Craving; yearning
20. Dead when delivered from the womb
21. Hand tool with a sharp, wedged blade
22. Deceived

Down
2. Having or showing religious devotion
4. Shrub with showy flowers of pink, white, or purple
5. Persons addicted to some activity or habit
6. Gloomy; dismal
8. Lot; group
10. Partial or total loss of memory caused by brain injury or shock
12. To a great degree
14. Deep narrow passes between steep heights
16. Comfort
17. Pestered
18. Causing a feeling of horror; ugly; unpleasant
19. Showing high moral qualities

Walk Two Moons Vocabulary Crossword 3

Across
1. Grating; easily irritated; rough
3. White sterol found in animal fats. Excessive amounts can cause blocked arteries.
8. Top of a pointed, tapering object or structure, as a mountain peak
12. Legal; proper; within the law
13. In a state of violent or destructive rage or frenzy
14. Having or showing religious devotion
16. Partial or total loss of memory caused by brain injury or shock
17. Mischievous
20. Demise, destruction or decay
21. Craving; yearning
22. Plentiful

Down
2. Dead when delivered from the womb
4. Causing a feeling of horror; ugly; unpleasant
5. Gloomy; dismal
6. Set or fixed firmly
7. Having the tendency to expect the best outcome
8. Refrain from troubling or worrying
9. Intense, periodically returning headache
10. Lot; group
11. Knotty & twisted, as in the trunk of an old tree
15. Not easily convinced or persuaded; doubtful
16. Surprise attack from hidden assailants
18. Divine aids; spiritual sustenance
19. Showing high moral qualities

Walk Two Moons Vocabulary Crossword 3 Answer Key

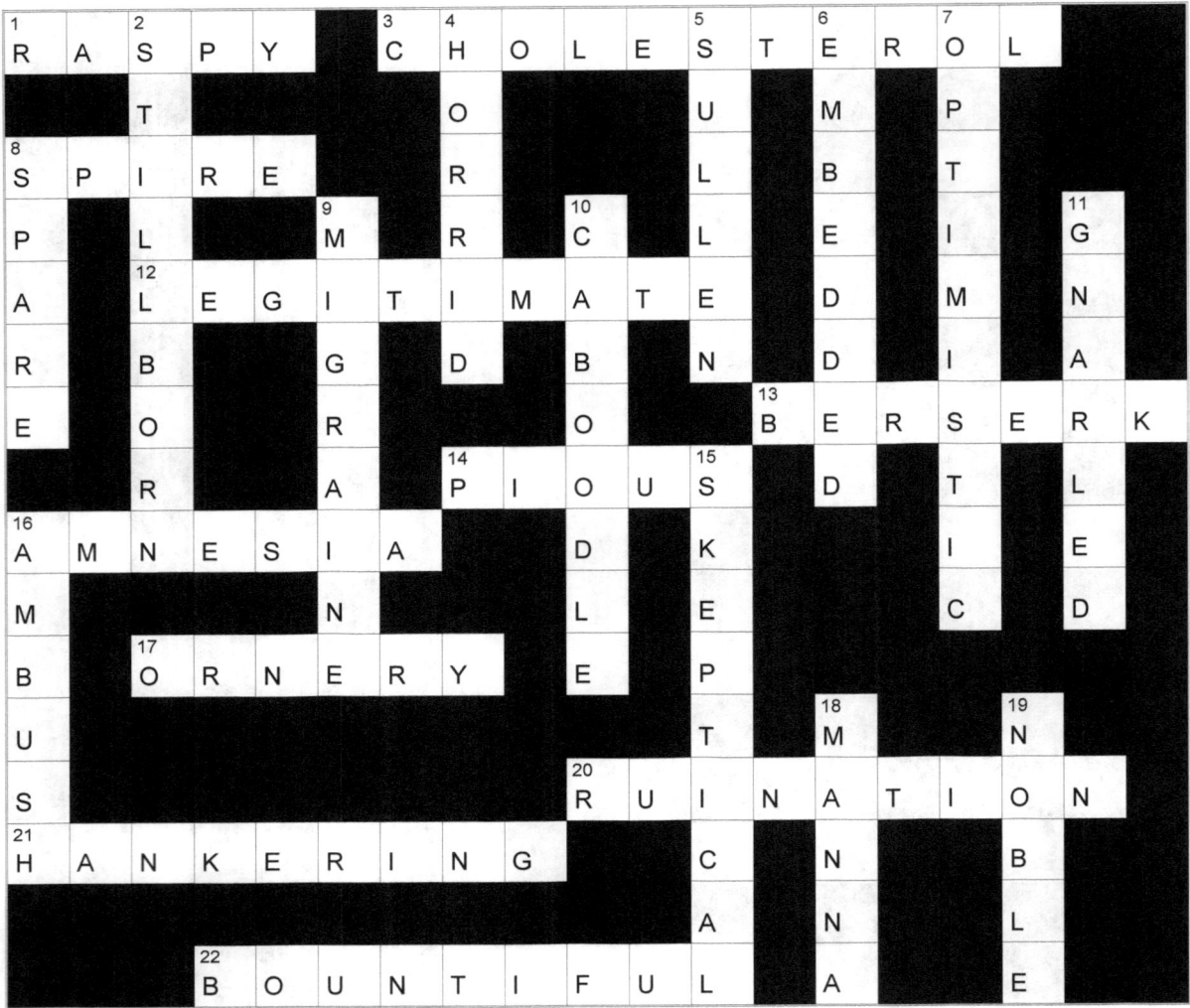

Across
1. Grating; easily irritated; rough
3. White sterol found in animal fats. Excessive amounts can cause blocked arteries.
8. Top of a pointed, tapering object or structure, as a mountain peak
12. Legal; proper; within the law
13. In a state of violent or destructive rage or frenzy
14. Having or showing religious devotion
16. Partial or total loss of memory caused by brain injury or shock
17. Mischievous
20. Demise, destruction or decay
21. Craving; yearning
22. Plentiful

Down
2. Dead when delivered from the womb
4. Causing a feeling of horror; ugly; unpleasant
5. Gloomy; dismal
6. Set or fixed firmly
7. Having the tendency to expect the best outcome
8. Refrain from troubling or worrying
9. Intense, periodically returning headache
10. Lot; group
11. Knotty & twisted, as in the trunk of an old tree
15. Not easily convinced or persuaded; doubtful
16. Surprise attack from hidden assailants
18. Divine aids; spiritual sustenance
19. Showing high moral qualities

Walk Two Moons Vocabulary Crossword 4

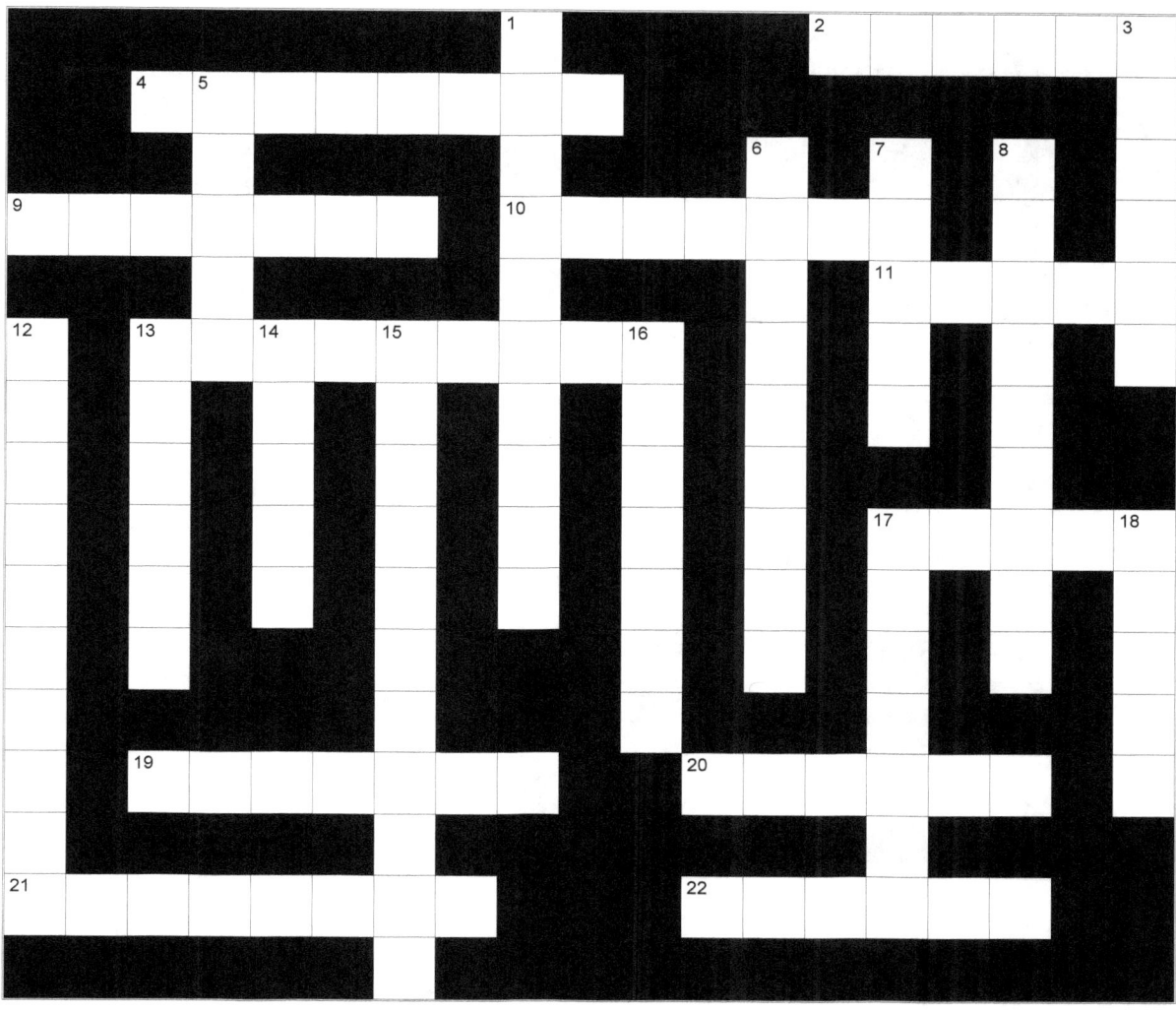

Across
2. Persons addicted to some activity or habit
4. Set or fixed firmly
9. Adapting a young child or animal to go without something
10. In Greek mythology, the first mortal woman; out o curiosity she opens a box
11. Top of a pointed, tapering object or structure, as a mountain peak
13. Craving; yearning
17. Having or showing religious devotion
19. Dead body
20. Surprise attack from hidden assailants
21. Lot; group
22. Breakfast cereal like granola

Down
1. Giving up hope
3. Gloomy; dismal
5. Divine aids; spiritual sustenance
6. Plentiful
7. Grating; easily irritated; rough
8. Dead when delivered from the womb
12. Having the tendency to expect the best outcome
13. Causing a feeling of horror; ugly; unpleasant
14. Showing high moral qualities
15. To a great degree
16. Knotty & twisted, as in the trunk of an old tree
17. Epidemic diseases that are deadly
18. Refrain from troubling or worrying

Walk Two Moons Vocabulary Crossword 4 Answer Key

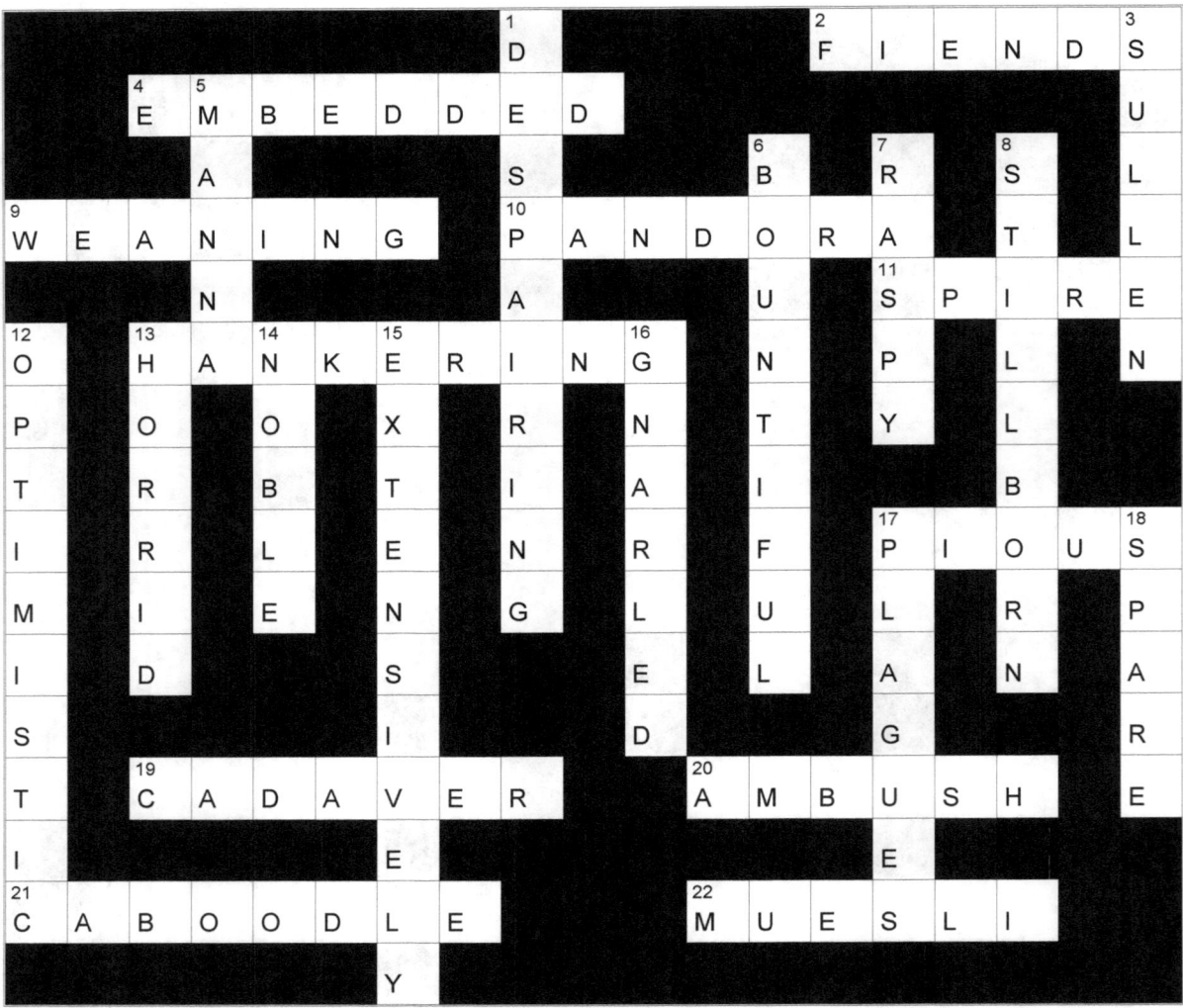

Across
2. Persons addicted to some activity or habit
4. Set or fixed firmly
9. Adapting a young child or animal to go without something
10. In Greek mythology, the first mortal woman; out o curiosity she opens a box
11. Top of a pointed, tapering object or structure, as a mountain peak
13. Craving; yearning
17. Having or showing religious devotion
19. Dead body
20. Surprise attack from hidden assailants
21. Lot; group
22. Breakfast cereal like granola

Down
1. Giving up hope
3. Gloomy; dismal
5. Divine aids; spiritual sustenance
6. Plentiful
7. Grating; easily irritated; rough
8. Dead when delivered from the womb
12. Having the tendency to expect the best outcome
13. Causing a feeling of horror; ugly; unpleasant
14. Showing high moral qualities
15. To a great degree
16. Knotty & twisted, as in the trunk of an old tree
17. Epidemic diseases that are deadly
18. Refrain from troubling or worrying

Walk Two Moons Vocabulary Juggle Lettters 1

1. MNOPTTINOE = 1. _____
   Having unlimited power

2. DRAEEYTB = 2. _____
   Deceived

3. ETORHESMUP = 3. _____
   Titan in Greek mythology who steals fire from heaven for the benefit of mankind

4. UMNYOANOS = 4. _____
   Given or written by a person whose name is unknown

5. YNDGEIF = 5. _____
   Challenging; daring

6. AERECTHOSUR = 6. _____
   Dangerously unstable

7. ENEYLXISTVE = 7. _____
   To a great degree

8. GTLIATMIEE = 8. _____
   Legal; proper; within the law

9. SAUHMB = 9. _____
   Surprise attack from hidden assailants

10. EONOSLC =10. _____
    Comfort

11. SSADEDIU =11. _____
    Persuade against (an action)

12. OBLEN =12. _____
    Showing high moral qualities

13. EFIEDSVNE =13. _____
    Feeling under attack and hence quick to justify one's actions

14. APELTICSK =14. _____
    Not easily convinced or persuaded; doubtful

Walk Two Moons Vocabulary Juggle Lettters 1 Answer Key

1. MNOPTTINOE = 1. OMNIPOTENT
   Having unlimited power

2. DRAEEYTB = 2. BETRAYED
   Deceived

3. ETORHESMUP = 3. PROMETHEUS
   Titan in Greek mythology who steals fire from heaven for the benefit of mankind

4. UMNYOANOS = 4. ANONYMOUS
   Given or written by a person whose name is unknown

5. YNDGEIF = 5. DEFYING
   Challenging; daring

6. AERECTHOSUR = 6. TREACHEROUS
   Dangerously unstable

7. ENEYLXISTVE = 7. EXTENSIVELY
   To a great degree

8. GTLIATMIEE = 8. LEGITIMATE
   Legal; proper; within the law

9. SAUHMB = 9. AMBUSH
   Surprise attack from hidden assailants

10. EONOSLC = 10. CONSOLE
    Comfort

11. SSADEDIU = 11. DISSUADE
    Persuade against (an action)

12. OBLEN = 12. NOBLE
    Showing high moral qualities

13. EFIEDSVNE = 13. DEFENSIVE
    Feeling under attack and hence quick to justify one's actions

14. APELTICSK = 14. SKEPTICAL
    Not easily convinced or persuaded; doubtful

Walk Two Moons Vocabulary Juggle Lettters 2

1. IICOALDB = 1. _____
   Very wicked or cruel

2. ETROAVCD = 2. _____
   Pranced

3. RSEMPHOUET = 3. _____
   Titan in Greek mythology who steals fire from heaven for the benefit of mankind

4. IHDROR = 4. _____
   Causing a feeling of horror; ugly; unpleasant

5. ONSNAMOYU = 5. _____
   Given or written by a person whose name is unknown

6. EDMDEDEB = 6. _____
   Set or fixed firmly

7. VELNLMEAOT = 7. _____
   Wishing evil or harm to others

8. CCONSISMA = 8. _____
   Soft, heelless, leather slippers originally worn by North American Indians

9. IVTYSELXNEE = 9. _____
   To a great degree

10. ROENRY = 10. _____
    Mischievous

11. EOADLBOC = 11. _____
    Lot; group

12. OLHLETSROEC = 12. _____
    White sterol found in animal fats. Excessive amounts can cause blocked arteries.

13. IFDSNE = 13. _____
    Persons addicted to some activity or habit

14. IARPHIN = 14. _____
    U-shaped

Walk Two Moons Vocabulary Juggle Lettters 2 Answer Key

1. IICOALDB = 1. DIABOLIC
Very wicked or cruel

2. ETROAVCD = 2. CAVORTED
Pranced

3. RSEMPHOUET = 3. PROMETHEUS
Titan in Greek mythology who steals fire from heaven for the benefit of mankind

4. IHDROR = 4. HORRID
Causing a feeling of horror; ugly; unpleasant

5. ONSNAMOYU = 5. ANONYMOUS
Given or written by a person whose name is unknown

6. EDMDEDEB = 6. EMBEDDED
Set or fixed firmly

7. VELNLMEAOT = 7. MALEVOLENT
Wishing evil or harm to others

8. CCONSISMA = 8. MOCCASINS
Soft, heelless, leather slippers originally worn by North American Indians

9. IVTYSELXNEE = 9. EXTENSIVELY
To a great degree

10. ROENRY = 10. ORNERY
Mischievous

11. EOADLBOC = 11. CABOODLE
Lot; group

12. OLHLETSROEC = 12. CHOLESTEROL
White sterol found in animal fats. Excessive amounts can cause blocked arteries.

13. IFDSNE = 13. FIENDS
Persons addicted to some activity or habit

14. IARPHIN = 14. HAIRPIN
U-shaped

Walk Two Moons Vocabulary Juggle Letters 3

1. AGRHNIKEN = 1. _____
   Craving; yearning

2. IRCUCAL = 2. _____
   Of supreme importance

3. NAANM = 3. _____
   Divine aids; spiritual sustenance

4. RESIP = 4. _____
   Top of a pointed, tapering object or structure, as a mountain peak

5. PSNIDERGIA = 5. _____
   Giving up hope

6. ENELSXIEVYT = 6. _____
   To a great degree

7. ITOIPCTIMS = 7. _____
   Having the tendency to expect the best outcome

8. SCOLNEO = 8. _____
   Comfort

9. STLHERO = 9. _____
   Pistol holder

10. EBTYDREA = 10. _____
    Deceived

11. ESOHCTRLEOL = 11. _____
    White sterol found in animal fats. Excessive amounts can cause blocked arteries.

12. HLCSEI = 12. _____
    Hand tool with a sharp, wedged blade

13. INCAEFDE = 13. _____
    Bold resistance to authority

14. ODHDRNDOROEN = 14. _____
    Shrub with showy flowers of pink, white, or purple

Walk Two Moons Vocabulary Juggle Letters 3 Answer Key

1. AGRHNIKEN = 1. HANKERING
   Craving; yearning

2. IRCUCAL = 2. CRUCIAL
   Of supreme importance

3. NAANM = 3. MANNA
   Divine aids; spiritual sustenance

4. RESIP = 4. SPIRE
   Top of a pointed, tapering object or structure, as a mountain peak

5. PSNIDERGIA = 5. DESPAIRING
   Giving up hope

6. ENELSXIEVYT = 6. EXTENSIVELY
   To a great degree

7. ITOIPCTIMS = 7. OPTIMISTIC
   Having the tendency to expect the best outcome

8. SCOLNEO = 8. CONSOLE
   Comfort

9. STLHERO = 9. HOLSTER
   Pistol holder

10. EBTYDREA = 10. BETRAYED
    Deceived

11. ESOHCTRLEOL = 11. CHOLESTEROL
    White sterol found in animal fats. Excessive amounts can cause blocked arteries.

12. HLCSEI = 12. CHISEL
    Hand tool with a sharp, wedged blade

13. INCAEFDE = 13. DEFIANCE
    Bold resistance to authority

14. ODHDRNDOROEN = 14. RHODODENDRON
    Shrub with showy flowers of pink, white, or purple

Walk Two Moons Vocabulary Juggle Letters 4

1. MUBAHS = 1. _____
   Surprise attack from hidden assailants

2. HAYLGST = 2. _____
   Horrible; frightful

3. OOSECLRHLTE = 3. _____
   White sterol found in animal fats. Excessive amounts can cause blocked arteries.

4. JUDESRNTGEPM = 4. _____
   Judgments without all the evidence

5. RDVEDIPE = 5. _____
   To have undergone a loss; to not have something

6. ANUSORATNKCE = 6. _____
   Quarrelsome

7. GALNMEIR = 7. _____
   Pretend to be ill to escape work

8. CLEUMSINLSAOE = 8. _____
   Varied; mixed

9. RUUFNMOLLY = 9. _____
   Sadly

10. TUUEADCCLMA =10. _____
    Collected or gathered together

11. SRPAY =11. _____
    Grating; easily irritated; rough

12. LEUNARCTT =12. _____
    Unwilling; hesitant

13. NNTIURAIO =13. _____
    Demise, destruction or decay

14. VARDOCTE =14. _____
    Pranced

Walk Two Moons Vocabulary Juggle Letters 4 Answer Key

1. MUBAHS = 1. AMBUSH
   Surprise attack from hidden assailants

2. HAYLGST = 2. GHASTLY
   Horrible; frightful

3. OOSECLRHLTE = 3. CHOLESTEROL
   White sterol found in animal fats. Excessive amounts can cause blocked arteries.

4. JUDESRNTGEPM = 4. PREJUDGMENTS
   Judgments without all the evidence

5. RDVEDIPE = 5. DEPRIVED
   To have undergone a loss; to not have something

6. ANUSORATNKCE = 6. CANTANKEROUS
   Quarrelsome

7. GALNMEIR = 7. MALINGER
   Pretend to be ill to escape work

8. CLEUMSINLSAOE = 8. MISCELLANEOUS
   Varied; mixed

9. RUUFNMOLLY = 9. MOURNFULLY
   Sadly

10. TUUEADCCLMA = 10. ACCUMULATED
    Collected or gathered together

11. SRPAY = 11. RASPY
    Grating; easily irritated; rough

12. LEUNARCTT = 12. RELUCTANT
    Unwilling; hesitant

13. NNTIURAIO = 13. RUINATION
    Demise, destruction or decay

14. VARDOCTE = 14. CAVORTED
    Pranced

ACCUMULATED	Collected or gathered together
AMBUSH	Surprise attack from hidden assailants
AMNESIA	Partial or total loss of memory caused by brain injury or shock
ANONYMOUS	Given or written by a person whose name is unknown
BADGERED	Pestered

BERSERK	In a state of violent or destructive rage or frenzy
BESIEGING	Harassing
BETRAYED	Deceived
BOUNTIFUL	Plentiful
CABOODLE	Lot; group

CADAVER	Dead body
CANTANKEROUS	Quarrelsome
CAPTIVE	One taken or held prisoner
CAVORTED	Pranced
CHISEL	Hand tool with a sharp, wedged blade

CHOLESTEROL	White sterol found in animal fats. Excessive amounts can cause blocked arteries.
COLOSSAL	Huge; gigantic
CONSOLE	Comfort
CRUCIAL	Of supreme importance
DEFENSIVE	Feeling under attack and hence quick to justify one's actions

DEFIANCE	Bold resistance to authority
DEFYING	Challenging; daring
DEPRIVED	To have undergone a loss; to not have something
DESPAIRING	Giving up hope
DIABOLIC	Very wicked or cruel

DISSUADE	Persuade against (an action)
ELABORATE	Add more details
EMBEDDED	Set or fixed firmly
EXTENSIVELY	To a great degree
FIENDS	Persons addicted to some activity or habit

FRAGILE	Physically weak; delicate
GHASTLY	Horrible; frightful
GNARLED	Knotty & twisted, as in the trunk of an old tree
GORGES	Deep narrow passes between steep heights
HAIRPIN	U-shaped

HANKERING	Craving; yearning
HOLSTER	Pistol holder
HORRID	Causing a feeling of horror; ugly; unpleasant
HYPNOTIZED	Put into a trance-like condition
IMPULSE	An impelling force, usually from within

INTRIGUING	Exciting interest of curiosity
LEGITIMATE	Legal; proper; within the law
MALEVOLENT	Wishing evil or harm to others
MALINGER	Pretend to be ill to escape work
MANNA	Divine aids; spiritual sustenance

MIGRAINE	Intense, periodically returning headache
MISCELLANEOUS	Varied; mixed
MOCCASINS	Soft, heelless, leather slippers originally worn by North American Indians
MOURNFULLY	Sadly
MUESLI	Breakfast cereal like granola

NOBLE	Showing high moral qualities
OMNIPOTENT	Having unlimited power
OPTIMISTIC	Having the tendency to expect the best outcome
ORNERY	Mischievous
PANDEMONIUM	Wild disorder, noise, or confusion

PANDORA	In Greek mythology, the first mortal woman; out o curiosity she opens a box
PERCOLATING	Bubbling up
PIOUS	Having or showing religious devotion
PLAGUES	Epidemic diseases that are deadly
PREJUDGMENTS	Judgments without all the evidence

PROMETHEUS	Titan in Greek mythology who steals fire from heaven for the benefit of mankind
RASPY	Grating; easily irritated; rough
REASSURANCE	Restored confidence
RELUCTANT	Unwilling; hesitant
RHODODENDRON	Shrub with showy flowers of pink, white, or purple

RUINATION	Demise, destruction or decay
RUMMAGING	Searching thoroughly by moving the contents about
SKEPTICAL	Not easily convinced or persuaded; doubtful
SPARE	Refrain from troubling or worrying
SPIRE	Top of a pointed, tapering object or structure, as a mountain peak

STILLBORN	Dead when delivered from the womb
SULLEN	Gloomy; dismal
TENTATIVELY	Hesitantly
TREACHEROUS	Dangerously unstable
UNADULTERATED	Pure

WEANING	Adapting a young child or animal to go without something

Walk Two Moons Vocabulary

DEFENSIVE	TREACHEROUS	SPARE	MOCCASINS	MALEVOLENT
BADGERED	NOBLE	GNARLED	TENTATIVELY	AMNESIA
RELUCTANT	DISSUADE	FREE SPACE	ELABORATE	GORGES
PROMETHEUS	SKEPTICAL	HAIRPIN	DESPAIRING	CHISEL
BETRAYED	PREJUDGMENTS	REASSURANCE	DEPRIVED	GHASTLY

Walk Two Moons Vocabulary

RUMMAGING	RASPY	BESIEGING	EMBEDDED	ANONYMOUS
HOLSTER	DEFIANCE	CANTANKEROUS	WEANING	FRAGILE
ORNERY	FIENDS	FREE SPACE	CONSOLE	CAPTIVE
UNADULTERATED	COLOSSAL	MISCELLANEOUS	HANKERING	MIGRAINE
IMPULSE	ACCUMULATED	HORRID	MUESLI	OPTIMISTIC

Walk Two Moons Vocabulary

DISSUADE	DEFENSIVE	IMPULSE	RASPY	UNADULTERATED
BESIEGING	SULLEN	AMNESIA	GHASTLY	FRAGILE
PLAGUES	ELABORATE	FREE SPACE	COLOSSAL	HYPNOTIZED
GNARLED	CONSOLE	BADGERED	PANDORA	CANTANKEROUS
PIOUS	CHOLESTEROL	LEGITIMATE	AMBUSH	REASSURANCE

Walk Two Moons Vocabulary

SPARE	EMBEDDED	MALINGER	BERSERK	MOCCASINS
HOLSTER	ACCUMULATED	CHISEL	BOUNTIFUL	DESPAIRING
MANNA	DEPRIVED	FREE SPACE	HAIRPIN	STILLBORN
RUMMAGING	RHODODENDRON	ORNERY	DEFIANCE	RELUCTANT
DEFYING	INTRIGUING	CAPTIVE	EXTENSIVELY	PROMETHEUS

Walk Two Moons Vocabulary

FIENDS	BETRAYED	TENTATIVELY	STILLBORN	CAPTIVE
CABOODLE	MISCELLANEOUS	CAVORTED	RASPY	RUMMAGING
RELUCTANT	SPIRE	FREE SPACE	DESPAIRING	CANTANKEROUS
REASSURANCE	MALEVOLENT	PERCOLATING	BADGERED	HYPNOTIZED
HOLSTER	MOURNFULLY	MIGRAINE	PLAGUES	SULLEN

Walk Two Moons Vocabulary

HORRID	CHOLESTEROL	WEANING	BERSERK	DEFENSIVE
MANNA	COLOSSAL	DEFIANCE	OMNIPOTENT	EXTENSIVELY
RUINATION	NOBLE	FREE SPACE	ORNERY	DIABOLIC
MALINGER	GORGES	IMPULSE	MUESLI	DEPRIVED
ELABORATE	PROMETHEUS	CONSOLE	ANONYMOUS	UNADULTERATED

Walk Two Moons Vocabulary

DESPAIRING	GORGES	HANKERING	SPARE	RHODODENDRON
SPIRE	RUMMAGING	RELUCTANT	PREJUDGMENTS	MUESLI
PANDORA	DEFYING	FREE SPACE	PANDEMONIUM	TENTATIVELY
DISSUADE	MOURNFULLY	REASSURANCE	DEFIANCE	PIOUS
SULLEN	CRUCIAL	NOBLE	CADAVER	AMNESIA

Walk Two Moons Vocabulary

GNARLED	OMNIPOTENT	EXTENSIVELY	CAVORTED	HOLSTER
HAIRPIN	RASPY	CONSOLE	DIABOLIC	PLAGUES
BESIEGING	WEANING	FREE SPACE	BETRAYED	GHASTLY
MIGRAINE	DEFENSIVE	OPTIMISTIC	UNADULTERATED	CABOODLE
STILLBORN	ACCUMULATED	MISCELLANEOUS	PROMETHEUS	TREACHEROUS

Walk Two Moons Vocabulary

SKEPTICAL	CAPTIVE	CAVORTED	HYPNOTIZED	OPTIMISTIC
BERSERK	BOUNTIFUL	PLAGUES	RUMMAGING	COLOSSAL
AMNESIA	BETRAYED	FREE SPACE	REASSURANCE	EMBEDDED
ACCUMULATED	TENTATIVELY	TREACHEROUS	SPIRE	LEGITIMATE
NOBLE	ELABORATE	STILLBORN	MALINGER	DESPAIRING

Walk Two Moons Vocabulary

MALEVOLENT	OMNIPOTENT	ORNERY	MANNA	FIENDS
DEFYING	PERCOLATING	GORGES	DEFENSIVE	PIOUS
GNARLED	EXTENSIVELY	FREE SPACE	RUINATION	BADGERED
HOLSTER	CADAVER	CABOODLE	CRUCIAL	RASPY
MOCCASINS	MOURNFULLY	DIABOLIC	PANDEMONIUM	HORRID

Walk Two Moons Vocabulary

RELUCTANT	RUMMAGING	NOBLE	SULLEN	DEFIANCE
LEGITIMATE	HYPNOTIZED	CHOLESTEROL	DISSUADE	MOCCASINS
MALINGER	PLAGUES	FREE SPACE	CHISEL	CANTANKEROUS
EXTENSIVELY	PROMETHEUS	CAPTIVE	REASSURANCE	GHASTLY
FIENDS	RASPY	PREJUDGMENTS	GORGES	PANDEMONIUM

Walk Two Moons Vocabulary

DIABOLIC	HORRID	INTRIGUING	BERSERK	FRAGILE
GNARLED	OMNIPOTENT	STILLBORN	SPARE	SPIRE
ACCUMULATED	RUINATION	FREE SPACE	DESPAIRING	CRUCIAL
WEANING	PANDORA	AMBUSH	TREACHEROUS	SKEPTICAL
DEPRIVED	ANONYMOUS	OPTIMISTIC	AMNESIA	COLOSSAL

Walk Two Moons Vocabulary

IMPULSE	BESIEGING	SKEPTICAL	BETRAYED	CABOODLE
STILLBORN	REASSURANCE	HANKERING	MUESLI	HYPNOTIZED
TREACHEROUS	FRAGILE	FREE SPACE	SPARE	DEPRIVED
ELABORATE	MALEVOLENT	ACCUMULATED	MALINGER	PROMETHEUS
LEGITIMATE	SULLEN	NOBLE	CAPTIVE	EMBEDDED

Walk Two Moons Vocabulary

RHODODENDRON	HORRID	WEANING	INTRIGUING	PERCOLATING
HOLSTER	MIGRAINE	OMNIPOTENT	MOURNFULLY	RUMMAGING
ANONYMOUS	DEFIANCE	FREE SPACE	RASPY	MANNA
MISCELLANEOUS	RUINATION	DESPAIRING	PIOUS	CHISEL
CONSOLE	CAVORTED	BERSERK	ORNERY	DISSUADE

Walk Two Moons Vocabulary

CONSOLE	DEFENSIVE	RHODODENDRON	OPTIMISTIC	RELUCTANT
IMPULSE	STILLBORN	CAPTIVE	CHISEL	SKEPTICAL
CAVORTED	DEFYING	FREE SPACE	ACCUMULATED	RASPY
HANKERING	WEANING	ANONYMOUS	TREACHEROUS	AMBUSH
PROMETHEUS	GNARLED	MUESLI	DIABOLIC	MOURNFULLY

Walk Two Moons Vocabulary

RUMMAGING	SPARE	FRAGILE	OMNIPOTENT	SPIRE
SULLEN	CABOODLE	CANTANKEROUS	BETRAYED	COLOSSAL
MALINGER	FIENDS	FREE SPACE	HOLSTER	ELABORATE
UNADULTERATED	NOBLE	AMNESIA	TENTATIVELY	MANNA
MALEVOLENT	PANDORA	DISSUADE	REASSURANCE	EMBEDDED

Walk Two Moons Vocabulary

IMPULSE	DEFYING	CANTANKEROUS	RUINATION	RELUCTANT
TREACHEROUS	MOCCASINS	INTRIGUING	DIABOLIC	MIGRAINE
DEPRIVED	EMBEDDED	FREE SPACE	FRAGILE	MOURNFULLY
MUESLI	WEANING	OMNIPOTENT	ANONYMOUS	PLAGUES
DEFIANCE	GHASTLY	TENTATIVELY	DESPAIRING	SKEPTICAL

Walk Two Moons Vocabulary

HOLSTER	PIOUS	CABOODLE	CHOLESTEROL	CRUCIAL
AMBUSH	CONSOLE	PERCOLATING	SULLEN	DEFENSIVE
REASSURANCE	MANNA	FREE SPACE	NOBLE	HORRID
CAVORTED	RASPY	BERSERK	MALEVOLENT	MISCELLANEOUS
CAPTIVE	SPIRE	UNADULTERATED	ELABORATE	HAIRPIN

Walk Two Moons Vocabulary

PANDEMONIUM	MISCELLANEOUS	AMBUSH	HOLSTER	PREJUDGMENTS
HANKERING	RUINATION	EXTENSIVELY	BERSERK	COLOSSAL
CAPTIVE	CADAVER	FREE SPACE	REASSURANCE	AMNESIA
BOUNTIFUL	HYPNOTIZED	SKEPTICAL	OMNIPOTENT	DEFENSIVE
FIENDS	PROMETHEUS	ORNERY	HORRID	DISSUADE

Walk Two Moons Vocabulary

DEPRIVED	MALEVOLENT	FRAGILE	SPIRE	DEFYING
PIOUS	HAIRPIN	BETRAYED	SULLEN	GNARLED
ELABORATE	DESPAIRING	FREE SPACE	LEGITIMATE	PLAGUES
ANONYMOUS	WEANING	BESIEGING	CHOLESTEROL	CABOODLE
GORGES	MOURNFULLY	MALINGER	INTRIGUING	UNADULTERATED

Walk Two Moons Vocabulary

DIABOLIC	MUESLI	COLOSSAL	BETRAYED	ORNERY
LEGITIMATE	PANDORA	RUINATION	ANONYMOUS	GHASTLY
GORGES	MOCCASINS	FREE SPACE	HYPNOTIZED	HANKERING
MANNA	AMBUSH	TENTATIVELY	FRAGILE	DEFYING
TREACHEROUS	NOBLE	OMNIPOTENT	PERCOLATING	WEANING

Walk Two Moons Vocabulary

MALINGER	CONSOLE	PROMETHEUS	FIENDS	MISCELLANEOUS
REASSURANCE	DEFENSIVE	UNADULTERATED	OPTIMISTIC	CRUCIAL
DEFIANCE	MALEVOLENT	FREE SPACE	EMBEDDED	EXTENSIVELY
ACCUMULATED	MOURNFULLY	RASPY	DEPRIVED	ELABORATE
AMNESIA	BERSERK	HOLSTER	BOUNTIFUL	CHISEL

Walk Two Moons Vocabulary

RUINATION	BADGERED	TENTATIVELY	REASSURANCE	CONSOLE
ELABORATE	MOURNFULLY	OPTIMISTIC	PANDEMONIUM	LEGITIMATE
DIABOLIC	CHISEL	FREE SPACE	RUMMAGING	PIOUS
HYPNOTIZED	DEFENSIVE	PREJUDGMENTS	INTRIGUING	COLOSSAL
MISCELLANEOUS	ACCUMULATED	UNADULTERATED	BOUNTIFUL	PERCOLATING

Walk Two Moons Vocabulary

PLAGUES	STILLBORN	CADAVER	CRUCIAL	FIENDS
MANNA	EXTENSIVELY	DEFIANCE	RASPY	OMNIPOTENT
HORRID	ORNERY	FREE SPACE	IMPULSE	MIGRAINE
WEANING	MALINGER	CAPTIVE	PROMETHEUS	PANDORA
SPARE	GORGES	FRAGILE	CHOLESTEROL	MALEVOLENT

Walk Two Moons Vocabulary

RHODODENDRON	COLOSSAL	DEPRIVED	CABOODLE	INTRIGUING
BADGERED	HOLSTER	HYPNOTIZED	OPTIMISTIC	GHASTLY
HAIRPIN	CANTANKEROUS	FREE SPACE	MOCCASINS	OMNIPOTENT
PERCOLATING	ORNERY	EMBEDDED	RUMMAGING	GORGES
MOURNFULLY	UNADULTERATED	CONSOLE	BOUNTIFUL	SPARE

Walk Two Moons Vocabulary

DEFENSIVE	ANONYMOUS	ELABORATE	MALEVOLENT	MIGRAINE
WEANING	CADAVER	PLAGUES	RASPY	MUESLI
SPIRE	CAVORTED	FREE SPACE	BERSERK	DEFIANCE
IMPULSE	EXTENSIVELY	CHISEL	HANKERING	LEGITIMATE
REASSURANCE	CRUCIAL	BESIEGING	RELUCTANT	SULLEN

Walk Two Moons Vocabulary

PANDORA	TREACHEROUS	DEFYING	FRAGILE	INTRIGUING
PANDEMONIUM	RUINATION	DISSUADE	MISCELLANEOUS	HORRID
CADAVER	GHASTLY	FREE SPACE	GORGES	MUESLI
AMBUSH	DIABOLIC	CHOLESTEROL	ORNERY	GNARLED
CAVORTED	PREJUDGMENTS	MIGRAINE	ANONYMOUS	ELABORATE

Walk Two Moons Vocabulary

PROMETHEUS	MOURNFULLY	WEANING	NOBLE	RASPY
DEFIANCE	SPIRE	STILLBORN	DEPRIVED	RUMMAGING
COLOSSAL	HAIRPIN	FREE SPACE	EMBEDDED	TENTATIVELY
BESIEGING	LEGITIMATE	SPARE	CANTANKEROUS	HANKERING
OMNIPOTENT	PIOUS	EXTENSIVELY	SKEPTICAL	HOLSTER

Walk Two Moons Vocabulary

HANKERING	MALINGER	COLOSSAL	BETRAYED	PANDORA
SULLEN	PERCOLATING	TREACHEROUS	MUESLI	RUMMAGING
DESPAIRING	DIABOLIC	FREE SPACE	CANTANKEROUS	MOCCASINS
PROMETHEUS	DEPRIVED	MOURNFULLY	HOLSTER	REASSURANCE
AMBUSH	DEFENSIVE	FIENDS	DEFIANCE	CHOLESTEROL

Walk Two Moons Vocabulary

OMNIPOTENT	BERSERK	BOUNTIFUL	EMBEDDED	FRAGILE
PREJUDGMENTS	OPTIMISTIC	GNARLED	HORRID	CAPTIVE
GHASTLY	PLAGUES	FREE SPACE	UNADULTERATED	WEANING
RELUCTANT	ELABORATE	CONSOLE	INTRIGUING	SPARE
MIGRAINE	EXTENSIVELY	CHISEL	STILLBORN	MALEVOLENT

Walk Two Moons Vocabulary

EXTENSIVELY	MALEVOLENT	TENTATIVELY	HORRID	DESPAIRING
OMNIPOTENT	NOBLE	PIOUS	REASSURANCE	STILLBORN
DEFENSIVE	HYPNOTIZED	FREE SPACE	MOCCASINS	MOURNFULLY
FRAGILE	SPIRE	PLAGUES	BOUNTIFUL	EMBEDDED
HOLSTER	PREJUDGMENTS	GORGES	SKEPTICAL	MUESLI

Walk Two Moons Vocabulary

ANONYMOUS	HAIRPIN	CAVORTED	SPARE	CONSOLE
CAPTIVE	CABOODLE	MIGRAINE	BESIEGING	DISSUADE
HANKERING	PERCOLATING	FREE SPACE	UNADULTERATED	DEFIANCE
RHODODENDRON	CADAVER	MANNA	FIENDS	AMBUSH
INTRIGUING	ACCUMULATED	RASPY	CANTANKEROUS	MALINGER